BOOKS BY DEBBIE MACOMBER

Any Dream Will Do
If Not for You
A Girl's Guide to Moving On
Last One Home

ROSE HARBOR INN

Sweet Tomorrows
Silver Linings
Love Letters
Rose Harbor in Bloom
The Inn at Rose Harbor

BLOSSOM STREET

Blossom Street Brides
Starting Now

CHRISTMAS NOVELS

Merry and Bright
Twelve Days of Christmas
Dashing Through the Snow
Mr. Miracle
Starry Night
Angels at the Table

For a complete list of books by Debbie Macomber, visit her website, debbiemacomber.com.

DEBBIE MACOMBER'S TABLE

DEBBIE MACOMBER'S TABLE

Sharing the Joy of Cooking

with Family and Friends

BALLANTINE BOOKS

NEW YORK

To my mother,
Rose "Connie" Adler (1922–2005),
who shared her love of food and cooking with me

CONTENTS

Introduction xi

Before You Use This Book 3

Breakfast 7

Appetizers and Snacks 35

Soups and Salads 49

Mains 71

Sides 111

Desserts 129

Drinks 165

Menus 181

Special Recipe Lists 187

Acknowledgments 193

Index 195

INTRODUCTION

It's said that two kinds of people exist in the world.

Those who eat to live.

And those who live to eat.

I don't think you'll need to guess which category I fall into!

In our family, food is much more than nourishment. It's love. It's appreciation. It's heritage. It's celebration. It's health and happiness, too. Anyone who reads my books is aware of how often I write about food. I've lost count of the number of times I've been asked for the recipe for Peggy Beldon's blueberry muffins. Or the peanut butter cookies that Jo Marie baked to welcome her guests at the Inn at Rose Harbor. Food says a lot about a character, and food helps to bring characters to life in the reader's mind—and in mine, too. We get to know people by the food they eat, and by their enjoyment of it. And you know what they say—"You are what you eat." In that case, pass the popcorn. (My personal weakness!)

Food is also an important part of my heritage. Many of the recipes in this cookbook are family staples passed down to me from my mother, recipes her own mother shared with her.

My mother was a phenomenal cook. She was a tiny woman, standing only four feet, eleven inches tall, weighing in at about 110 pounds. The most she ever weighed was when she was pregnant with me, topping the scales at 140 pounds. I've heard it said, "Don't trust a skinny cook." Well, whoever came up with that idea never met my mother! Although she was small, Mom knew her way around the kitchen.

Some of the fondest memories of my mother are ones that took place in the kitchen. We cooked together, laughed together, and shared recipes back and forth like they were top government secrets. Every conversation included something about food: What were we each cooking for dinner? Had I tried this recipe or that? It took us weeks to decide what side dishes to serve for our Thanksgiving dinner.

The kitchen became more than a stove and a refrigerator. It was a counseling center. Some of the most serious conversations I had with Mom took place in front of the kitchen countertop. Our kitchen was a dance hall, too. Mom and I often played music and bebopped around the island. It was the one room where the entire family gathered, sneaking bites of whatever it was Mom and I were cooking. I still have her recipe box from when she was a young wife, and it's one of my most treasured possessions.

Since Mom's passing, a generational shift has taken place. It's as lively and fun as it's always been in the kitchen, only now the recipe sharing and the dancing continue with my two daughters and two daughters-in-law. And again, some of the most meaningful conversations have taken place in the kitchen. One generation to the next and . . . to the next. Yes, the grandchildren often get involved in helping me prepare a meal. As we're putting together the ingredients for a recipe, the grandkids talk to me about school, their friends, and what's going on in their lives. Our grandsons enjoy working alongside me in the kitchen as much as our granddaughters. From the time they have been able to stand on a stepstool and reach the countertop, the grandkids have been whipping up recipes with me.

Why a cookbook, and why from me? I'm certainly not a professional chef. I've never attended a culinary school. Sure, I love to cook and eat, but that doesn't make me unusual. We all need nourishment, but to me, food is so much more. I am eager to share with you how food not only feeds the body but also the soul, with a lot of heart thrown in.

In this cookbook, I'm welcoming you into my home, into my kitchen, and into my life. My purpose is to share the many ways food touches each one of us. Food can be the helping hand we extend to a friend in need. It can be a way of showing our appreciation to those whose kindness touches us. It's a means of gathering family and friends together, providing them a chance to laugh and to share around the table. Food helps us to celebrate life's many occasions.

I'm delighted to share this collection of fun and delicious recipes with you.

I think my mom would be proud.

Debbie Macomber

DEBBIE MACOMBER'S TABLE

BEFORE YOU USE THIS BOOK

Many ingredients come in different forms: fresh or dried, salted or unsalted, small, medium, or large, coarse or fine, bleached or unbleached.

Unless a recipe says otherwise, all:

Eggs are large.

Flour is all-purpose. Bleached or unbleached is up to you.

Sugar is granulated. If the recipe calls for *brown sugar* and doesn't specify light or dark, use whatever you have on hand or whichever you prefer.

Butter is unsalted.

Cream is heavy or whipping cream.

Milk is whole milk. You can probably substitute 2% with good results, but I won't guarantee what a recipe will taste like if you use skim or nonfat.

Salt is kosher salt. If you use regular table salt, start with half the amount specified in the recipe and adjust the seasoning to your taste.

Pepper is freshly ground black pepper.

Cheese is full fat. You can use white or yellow Cheddar, whichever you prefer.

Scallions or *green onions* should always have the roots and tops trimmed. Unless otherwise noted, use both white and green parts.

Vegetable oil is any neutral-tasting vegetable oil, like canola or a mild olive oil.

The recipes give volume (cup, teaspoon, and tablespoon) measurements wherever possible. If you don't like having a half or quarter of an onion lying around, it's helpful to know that 1 small onion is about ½ cup; 1 medium onion is about 1 cup, and 1 large onion is about 2 cups.

If I know a substitution can successfully be made for an ingredient, the recipe or headnote will say so.

You can use butter or cooking spray to grease baking pans or muffin tins, whichever you prefer. I find it easier to use cooking spray on muffin tins, myself.

Several recipes call for toasted nuts or roasted garlic.

To toast nuts in the oven:

Preheat the oven to 350°F. Place the nuts in a single layer on a rimmed baking sheet and bake for 5 to 10 minutes, until the nuts are fragrant. Stir or shake the pan once or twice while the nuts are toasting.

Remove the pan from the oven and cool the nuts on a plate.

To toast nuts in the microwave:

Spread ½ cup nuts in a single layer in a microwave-safe dish. Add ½ teaspoon melted butter or oil. Stir to coat the nuts. Microwave for 1 minute. Stir and microwave for another minute. Continue to microwave in 1-minute increments, stirring after each time, until the nuts are lightly browned and fragrant.

To roast garlic:

Preheat the oven to 400°F. Slice off and discard the top third of a head of garlic so that each clove is exposed. Place on a piece of aluminum foil and drizzle the garlic with olive oil. Wrap up tightly in foil, place in the oven, and bake for 45 to 55 minutes, until the center cloves are soft when pierced with a knife. Let cool for 10 minutes.

BREAKFAST

I've always been a big fan of breakfast, because I'm a morning person. (Okay, the truth—I'm a fan of *every* meal.) When we were first married, Wayne asked me if I had to shine so brightly in the mornings. As I stated earlier, two kinds of people exist in this world: those who eat to live and those who live to eat. Well, I misspoke. There are also those who wake up and say, "Good morning, God!" and those who grouchily awaken to say, "Good God, it's morning." I doubt you'll have trouble figuring out which category Wayne falls into!

Even now, with an empty nest, I make sure Wayne and I have breakfast together the same way I did when the kids were living at home. When they were toddlers, I read classic children's books to them each morning during their breakfast. Then the hectic mornings of school began, getting them all ready for their day, but never without a good breakfast before they headed out the door.

My own mornings start early, usually before four or shortly thereafter. I know, I know—it's early. Those predawn hours begin with Bible reading and journal writing. I've kept a journal my entire life. I have three for each year: a personal journal, a gratitude journal, and a prayer journal. I write in each one every single day. This process usually takes about ninety minutes, and then I change into my swimsuit and head for the local community pool where I swim a half-mile. (Trust me, a half-mile is a lot farther in the water than on land!) Once I'm back home, I stir Wayne into the land of the living with coffee and the promise of breakfast.

Breakfast also played a key role when I developed the premise for the Inn at Rose Harbor series. I needed to find a way to bring the guests of Jo Marie's inn together so that the plots weren't random and disjointed. Those luscious breakfasts that Jo Marie created connected the characters in the series. Over juice, fruit, muffins, and coffee, the guests bonded during their morning conversations, the same way it happens in my home.

GRATITUDE BREAD

Makes 1 (8 x 4½-inch) loaf

Remember the friendship bread craze from a few years back? This is a different take on that idea. Giving a loaf of this delicious bread is a sweet way of expressing appreciation to those who have touched your life. I imagine this recipe is one Shay, from Any Dream Will Do, *would use to thank those who guided and helped her after her release from prison.*

Preheat the oven to 375°F. Butter an 8 x 4-inch loaf pan. Line the pan with parchment paper cut to fit the length of the pan with 2 inches hanging over the sides.

In a large bowl, whisk together the flour, sugar, baking powder, baking soda, and salt. Add the buttermilk, egg, butter, and vanilla, and stir with a rubber spatula just until combined.

Gently fold in your choice of mix-ins.

Pour the batter into the prepared pan and smooth the top. Bake for 55 to 65 minutes, until a knife inserted in the center comes out with a few crumbs attached.

Let the loaf cool in the pan for 10 minutes, then turn the loaf out onto a wire rack to cool. Slice and serve warm or at room temperature.

Mix-ins:

Northwest Mixed Berry: Fold in 1½ cups fresh or frozen mixed berries.

Peach Almond: Reduce the vanilla extract to ½ teaspoon and add ¾ teaspoon almond extract. Fold in 1 cup chopped peeled fresh peaches and ¾ cup chopped almonds.

Pear Walnut: Fold in 1 cup chopped fresh pears and ¾ cup chopped walnuts.

Cranberry Pecan: Fold in 1 cup dried cranberries and ¾ cup chopped pecans.

2 cups flour
⅔ cup sugar
1½ teaspoons baking powder
½ teaspoon baking soda
¾ teaspoon salt
1 cup buttermilk
1 egg
4 tablespoons (½ stick) butter, melted and cooled
1 teaspoon vanilla extract
Your choice of mix-ins (see below)

You can use any combination of fruits and nuts as long as you keep the proportion of 1 cup fruit to ¾ cup nuts. If you're only using fresh fruit, use 1½ cups per loaf.

This will keep, wrapped in plastic wrap or aluminum foil, for 3 days at room temperature or for 3 months frozen.

CHOCOLATE CHERRY QUICK BREAD

Makes 1 (9 x 5-inch) loaf

This moist loaf packed with cherries isn't overly sweet. And it's one way to have chocolate for breakfast! It's not a bad afternoon pick-me-up, either. Try it with a glass of ice-cold milk or a cup of strong coffee.

1¾ cups flour

⅓ cup unsweetened cocoa powder

1 teaspoon baking powder

½ teaspoon baking soda

½ teaspoon salt

2 (10-ounce) bags frozen pitted cherries, unthawed, 1 bag coarsely chopped

1 cup sugar

½ cup sour cream

3 eggs

6 tablespoons (¾ stick) butter, melted and cooled

Preheat the oven to 350°F. Grease a 9 x 5-inch loaf pan.

In a medium bowl, whisk together the flour, cocoa powder, baking powder, baking soda, and salt.

Empty the bag of whole cherries into a medium saucepan. Heat over medium heat for 3 to 4 minutes, until warmed. Add the sugar and use a potato masher to crush the cherries. Cook for 15 minutes, or until the mixture has reduced and thickened and is syrupy but chunky. Transfer the cherries to a large bowl and let cool for 10 minutes.

Whisk the sour cream and eggs into the mashed cherries, then stir in the melted butter. Stir in the flour mixture just until combined. Fold in the chopped cherries.

Pour the batter into the prepared loaf pan. Bake for about 1 hour, until a knife or toothpick inserted in the center comes out clean.

Let the bread cool in the pan for 15 minutes, then turn it out onto a wire rack to cool completely.

You can use either Dutch process or natural cocoa here. Using frozen cherries means you can enjoy this all year round.

Wrapped in plastic wrap or aluminum foil, this will keep for 3 days at room temperature or for up to 3 months frozen.

CINNAMON STREUSEL COFFEE COFFEE CAKE

Serves 8

This coffee-scented cake can be on the table in an hour and makes breakfast or snack time something special. It makes for a great midnight snack. And besides, coffee cake made with actual coffee only makes sense.

Preheat the oven to 350°F. Grease an 8 x 8-inch baking pan.

Make the cake:

In a medium bowl, whisk together the flour, baking powder, and salt.

In a small bowl, whisk together the milk, instant coffee, and vanilla.

In a large bowl, cream together the butter and sugar with an electric hand mixer on high until light and fluffy, about 2 minutes. Add the egg and mix well. Add half of the flour mixture and mix just until combined. Now add all of the milk mixture and mix just until combined. Finally, add the rest of the flour and mix just until combined.

Make the streusel:

In a medium bowl, combine the butter, flour, brown sugar, cinnamon, and salt. Blend with a fork until combined and crumbly.

Pour half of the batter into the prepared pan and spread it out evenly with an offset spatula. Sprinkle half of the streusel mixture evenly over the batter. Spread the remaining batter in the pan and sprinkle the remaining streusel over the top.

Bake for 45 to 55 minutes, until a knife inserted in the center comes out clean. Place the pan on a wire rack to cool for 10 minutes. Serve warm or at room temperature.

Cake:
2 cups flour
2 teaspoons baking powder
¼ teaspoon salt
¾ cup milk
1 tablespoon instant coffee granules
1 teaspoon vanilla extract
½ cup (1 stick) butter, at room temperature
¾ cup sugar
1 egg

Streusel:
½ cup (1 stick) butter, at room temperature
1 cup flour
1 cup brown sugar
1 tablespoon ground cinnamon
¼ teaspoon salt

BLUEBERRY CRUMB CAKE

Serves 8 to 10

Bursting with juicy fruit and topped with buttery cinnamon-scented crumbs, this simple cake is a summertime treat. This is our oldest grandson, Cameron's, favorite cake. He loves blueberries and so do I.

Preheat the oven to 375°F. Grease a 9-inch round cake pan.

Make the cake:

In a large bowl, whisk together the flour, sugar, baking powder, and salt. Make a well in the center.

In a medium bowl, whisk together the butter, eggs, vanilla, and milk. Add all at once to the dry ingredients and stir just until combined. Gently fold in the blueberries. Spread the batter evenly in the prepared pan.

Make the crumb topping:

In a small bowl, use a fork to combine all the crumb topping ingredients until clumps form. Sprinkle evenly over the batter.

Bake for 45 to 55 minutes, until light golden brown and a knife inserted in the center comes out clean. Place the pan on a wire rack to cool. Slice and serve warm or at room temperature.

Cake:
2 cups flour

1 cup sugar

2 teaspoons baking powder

¾ teaspoon salt

½ cup (1 stick) butter, melted and cooled

2 eggs

1½ teaspoons vanilla extract

½ cup milk

2 cups fresh blueberries

Crumb topping:
6 tablespoons (¾ stick) butter, at room temperature

¾ cup flour

¾ cup sugar

¾ teaspoon ground cinnamon

¼ teaspoon salt

OVERNIGHT CARAMEL PECAN ROLLS

Serves 6

Make these gooey treats the night before for a weekend breakfast or brunch. They make a lovely welcome gift for new neighbors or for a new mother.

1 cup pecan halves or pieces
½ cup (1 stick) butter
¾ cup brown sugar
3 tablespoons light corn syrup
¼ teaspoon salt
12 frozen yeast rolls, such as Rhodes Yeast Dinner Rolls

A nonstick pan makes turning out the rolls easier, but if you don't have one, just grease or spray the pan very well.

Spread the pecans in an even layer over a 9-inch round nonstick baking pan with sides at least 1½ inches high. Spray the pan with cooking spray.

In a medium saucepan, combine the butter, brown sugar, corn syrup, and salt and heat over medium heat until the brown sugar is dissolved but not boiling. Pour the mixture over the pecans and let cool for 10 minutes.

Place the frozen yeast rolls on top of the pecans and syrup. Spray a piece of plastic wrap large enough to cover the pan completely with cooking spray. Cover the pan loosely and let the rolls rise at room temperature for at least 8 hours but no more than 12 hours.

Preheat the oven to 350°F.

Remove the plastic wrap and bake the rolls for 30 minutes, or until puffed and golden brown. Remove the pan from the oven. Place your serving plate upside down on top of the rolls and invert the rolls onto the serving plate. Serve warm.

MUFFIN TIN DONUT HOLES

Makes 48

These sweet morsels are quicker to make than donuts, and healthier, as they're baked instead of fried. They are rolled in melted butter and cinnamon sugar after they're baked, giving them the classic taste of a cake donut. They're yummy, too.

Preheat the oven to 400°F. Grease or spray with cooking spray two 24-hole mini muffin tins.

Make the donut holes:

In a large bowl, whisk together the flour, sugar, cornstarch, baking powder, salt, and nutmeg. In a separate bowl, whisk together the buttermilk and eggs. Add the buttermilk and eggs to the flour mixture and lightly mix together. Add the melted butter and mix just until combined.

Scoop a heaping tablespoon of batter into each well of the muffin tins. Bake for 10 to 13 minutes, until the donuts are still pale but a toothpick inserted in the center of a donut comes out clean.

Make the coating:

While the donuts are baking, in a medium bowl, whisk together the sugar and cinnamon.

Remove the donuts from the oven and place on a wire rack to cool for 5 minutes before removing from the tins.

Brush each donut all over with the melted butter, then roll in the cinnamon-sugar mixture. Transfer to a serving platter as you finish each donut. Serve warm or at room temperature.

Donut holes:

2¾ cups flour

½ cup sugar

¼ cup cornstarch

1 tablespoon baking powder

1 teaspoon salt

¼ teaspoon ground nutmeg

1 cup buttermilk

3 eggs

½ cup (1 stick) butter, melted and cooled

Coating:

1 cup sugar

2 teaspoons ground cinnamon

½ cup (1 stick) butter, melted

These are best served on the day that they are made. You can freeze the uncoated donut holes for up to 1 month. Defrost them at room temperature, then dip in the butter and cinnamon-sugar mixture.

Do not use paper liners for these donuts. You can bake them in a regular-size muffin tin if you prefer. Just increase the baking time by a few minutes.

PUMPKIN APPLE CRUNCH MUFFINS

Makes 24

This is the perfect marriage of fall ingredients and flavors. These are best served the day they are made but will keep for three days before the topping loses its crunch.

Crunch topping:
½ cup (1 stick) cold butter, cubed
⅔ cup sugar
¼ cup flour
1 teaspoon ground cinnamon
⅛ teaspoon salt

Muffins:
2½ cups flour
2 cups sugar
1 teaspoon baking soda
1 teaspoon ground cinnamon
½ teaspoon ground nutmeg
¼ teaspoon ground cloves
¼ teaspoon salt
2 eggs
1¼ cups canned pumpkin puree (not pumpkin pie filling)
½ cup vegetable oil
2 cups chopped apples

These can be frozen up to 3 months. Thaw in the freezer bag on the counter overnight, then warm them in a low oven before serving.

Preheat the oven to 350°F. Grease or spray with cooking spray two 12-hole muffin tins.

Make the crunch topping:

In a medium bowl, mix together the butter, sugar, flour, cinnamon, and salt using a fork until crumbly.

Make the muffins:

In a large bowl, whisk together the flour, sugar, baking soda, cinnamon, nutmeg, cloves, and salt. Add the eggs, pumpkin puree, oil, and apples all at once. Mix until just combined. Fill the muffin tins two-thirds full with batter.

Sprinkle the streusel mixture evenly over the tops of the muffins.

Bake for 25 to 30 minutes, rotating the tins halfway through, until a toothpick inserted in the center comes out clean. Place the tins on wire racks to cool for 10 minutes. Remove the muffins from the pan and serve, or place them on the racks to cool completely.

STRAWBERRIES AND CREAM SCONES WITH STRAWBERRY BUTTER

Makes 8

Nothing says spring to me more than strawberries and cream. These would be lovely at a Mother's Day or Easter brunch. Serve on the same day for the best results.

Make the strawberry butter:

In a small bowl, use a fork to combine the butter, salt, and jam. Cover and refrigerate until ready to use.

Make the scones:

Preheat the oven to 400°F. Line a rimmed baking sheet with parchment paper.

In a medium bowl, whisk together the flour, sugar, baking powder, baking soda, and salt. Cut in the butter with a pastry cutter or two knives until crumbly.

In another medium bowl, whisk together 1 of the eggs, the milk, and the cream. Add the mixture all at once to the dry ingredients. Use a fork to combine just until moistened. Gently fold in the strawberries.

Turn the dough out onto a floured surface and press it into an 8-inch circle 1 inch thick. Cut into 8 even wedges and place on the prepared baking sheet, leaving at least 2 inches between each wedge. Lightly beat the remaining egg with 1 teaspoon water and brush the tops with the egg wash.

Bake the scones for 18 to 20 minutes, until golden brown. Cool on the baking sheet for 10 minutes.

Make the glaze:

In a small bowl, whisk together the powdered sugar, cream, and vanilla. Drizzle over the cooled scones.

Serve warm or at room temperature with the strawberry butter.

Strawberry butter:
½ cup (1 stick) butter, at room temperature
¼ teaspoon salt
¼ cup seedless strawberry jam

Scones:
2½ cups flour, plus more for dusting
⅓ cup sugar
2 teaspoons baking powder
½ teaspoon baking soda
½ teaspoon salt
½ cup (1 stick) very cold butter, cut into cubes
2 eggs
½ cup milk
2 tablespoons cream
1½ cups fresh strawberries, hulled and quartered

Glaze:
½ cup powdered sugar
5 teaspoons cream
½ teaspoon vanilla extract

The strawberry butter can be stored, tightly covered, in the refrigerator for 1 month, or 6 months in the freezer.

MAPLE PECAN SCONES WITH BACON MAPLE BUTTER

Makes 8

Scones are a great afternoon snack, and these go perfectly with a hot cup of tea or coffee, especially on a cool fall day. Sprinkle additional pecans on top before baking if you want extra crunch and nuttiness. They are best served the day they're made.

Bacon maple butter:
½ cup (1 stick) butter, at room temperature
3 tablespoons maple syrup
4 slices bacon, cooked, drained, and diced

Scones:
2 cups flour, plus more for dusting
⅓ cup brown sugar
1 tablespoon baking powder
½ teaspoon salt
½ cup (1 stick) cold butter, cubed
1 cup chopped pecans
1¼ teaspoons maple extract
¾ cup cream

Glaze:
¾ cup powdered sugar
3 tablespoons maple syrup
2 teaspoons cream

The maple butter can be stored, tightly covered, in the refrigerator for 1 month or 6 months in the freezer.

Make the bacon maple butter:

In a small bowl, use a fork to combine the butter and maple syrup. Stir in the bacon.

Make the scones:

Preheat the oven to 400°F. Line a rimmed baking sheet with aluminum foil or parchment paper.

In a large bowl, whisk together the flour, brown sugar, baking powder, and salt. Cut in the butter with a pastry cutter or two knives until crumbly. Stir in the pecans. Make a well in the center of the mixture and add the maple extract and cream all at once. Stir until almost fully combined. Do not overmix or the dough will be tough.

Turn the dough out onto a lightly floured surface and gently knead a few times until the dough comes together. Press the dough into an 8-inch circle about ½ inch thick and cut into 8 even wedges. Transfer the scones to the prepared baking sheet, leaving at least 2 inches between each wedge.

Bake the scones for 18 to 22 minutes, until light golden brown on top. Let cool on the baking sheet for 10 minutes.

Make the glaze:

In a small bowl, whisk together the powdered sugar, maple syrup, and cream until smooth. Drizzle over the cooled scones.

Serve warm or at room temperature with the bacon maple butter.

CREAM CHEESE DANISHES

Makes 12

Want something easy but impressive for a holiday breakfast or tea? These will dazzle your family and friends. For the best results, serve them on the same day you make them.

Preheat the oven to 375°F. Position two racks in the middle and bottom rungs of the oven. Line two rimmed baking sheets with parchment paper.

In a large bowl, cream together the cream cheese and sugar with an electric hand mixer on medium speed until very smooth. Mix in the vanilla.

On a lightly floured surface, unroll one tube of dough with a short side facing you. Pinch all the seams together. Lightly flour the top, then gently roll out the dough into a 9 x 12-inch rectangle. Pinch the seams together again. Cut 6 even strips, each measuring 1½ inches wide and 12 inches long. Twist each strip, leaving a 1-inch section flat at one end. With the flat end in the center, wrap the dough around itself into a loose pinwheel shape. Transfer to the prepared baking sheet. Repeat with the remaining strips of dough.

Repeat with the second tube of crescent roll dough.

In a small bowl, beat the egg with the water. Put a rounded tablespoon of filling into the center of each pastry. Brush all the exposed dough with egg wash.

Bake for 10 to 12 minutes, rotating the baking sheets from top to bottom halfway through, until the pastries are puffed and golden. Let cool for 5 minutes (the filling will be very hot) and serve.

6 ounces cream cheese, at room temperature

¼ cup plus 2 tablespoons sugar

1 teaspoon vanilla extract

Flour, for dusting

2 tubes refrigerated crescent roll dough

1 egg

1 teaspoon water

CHOCOLATE CRANBERRY CROISSANT PUDDING

Serves 4 to 5

This decadent bread pudding is a delicious addition to a holiday brunch menu. Make it the night before; it gets better as it sits.

8 mini croissants
⅓ cup semisweet chocolate chips
½ cup dried cranberries
½ cup sliced almonds
1 cup milk
½ cup cream
3 eggs
⅓ cup sugar
1 teaspoon vanilla extract

This recipe is easily doubled. Use a 9 x 13-inch pan and bake for another 5 to 10 minutes, until the middle is set.

Cut 6 of the croissants in half lengthwise. Set the tops aside. Cut the bottoms and the remaining croissants into cubes and place in an 8 x 8-inch baking dish.

Sprinkle the chocolate chips, then the cranberries, then ¼ cup of the sliced almonds over the croissants.

In a medium bowl, whisk together the milk, cream, eggs, sugar, and vanilla. Pour the mixture evenly over the croissants. Arrange the reserved croissant tops on top and press lightly into the liquid.

Sprinkle the remaining ¼ cup sliced almonds over the top. Cover the dish with plastic wrap and refrigerate for at least 2 hours or up to 12 hours.

Remove the baking dish from the refrigerator and remove the plastic wrap.

Preheat the oven to 350°F.

Bake the bread pudding for 30 to 35 minutes, until the pudding is set and the almonds are lightly toasted. Let cool for 10 minutes before serving. Serve warm or at room temperature.

LEMON RICOTTA PANCAKES

Makes about 30 (3-inch) pancakes

With a hint of bright lemon flavor, these pancakes are light and airy. Our favorite way to eat them is with fresh berries and whipped cream, but they go well with maple syrup, too.

Preheat the oven to 200°F. Place a rimmed baking sheet in the oven.

Heat a griddle over medium heat. Grease or spray it with cooking spray.

In a large bowl, whisk together the flour, baking soda, sugar, and salt.

In a medium bowl, whisk together the eggs, cheese, milk, butter, lemon zest, and lemon juice. Add the cheese mixture to the dry ingredients all at once and mix with a spoon or spatula until just combined.

Ladle the batter in 2-tablespoon portions onto the griddle. Cook until golden brown on the bottom, about 2 minutes, then flip and cook until the second side is browned. Repeat until all the batter is finished.

As the pancakes are finished, put them on the baking sheet in the oven. Serve hot.

1½ cups flour

1½ teaspoons baking soda

3 tablespoons sugar

¼ teaspoon salt

2 eggs

¾ cup ricotta cheese

1 cup milk

½ cup (1 stick) butter, melted and cooled

2 teaspoons lemon zest

1 tablespoon lemon juice

This can be made with 2% or skim milk, or any plant milk.

BAKED OATMEAL

Serves 8

My favorite form of exercise is swimming, and when I come home from the pool, there's nothing I like better than a hot bowl of oatmeal. This dish, which tastes like a warm oatmeal cookie, is one Jo Marie would enjoy serving her guests at the Inn at Rose Harbor, and one our grandson, Mason, enjoys, too.

Variations:

Banana Bread: 2½ cups bananas and ½ cup walnuts. Mix 1 teaspoon cinnamon with 4 teaspoons sugar and sprinkle evenly over the top.

Triple Berry Crisp: 2½ cups frozen mixed berries and ½ cup granola.

Granola: ⅔ cup raisins, ⅔ cup chopped apricots, ⅓ cup shredded coconut, ⅓ cup chopped pecans or walnuts

Apple Cinnamon: 3 cups peeled, sliced apples. Mix 1 teaspoon cinnamon with 4 teaspoons sugar and sprinkle evenly over the top.

Preheat the oven to 350°F.

In a large bowl, stir together the oats, brown sugar, baking powder, salt, and cinnamon.

In a separate bowl, whisk together the eggs, milk, and melted butter. Add to the oat mixture and stir until completely combined.

Pour the batter into a 9 x 13-inch baking pan and distribute your choice of toppings evenly over all.

Bake for 40 to 45 minutes, until golden brown and crispy around the edges. Let cool on a wire rack for 10 minutes. Serve warm.

6 cups rolled oats

1½ cups brown sugar

4 teaspoons baking powder

2 teaspoons salt

1 tablespoon ground cinnamon

4 eggs

3 cups milk

½ cup (1 stick) butter, melted and cooled

Your choice: 3 cups fresh or frozen fruit *or* 3 thickly sliced bananas *or* 2 cups chopped nuts *or* 2 cups chopped dried fruit

You can assemble this dish the night before and put it in the oven in the morning. Leftovers can be cut into squares and reheated, or eaten on the run at room temperature.

You can use light or dark brown sugar, but don't substitute quick-cooking or instant oatmeal.

BISCUITS AND GRAVY

Makes 8 biscuits and a little more than 2 cups gravy

You know what they say about the way to a man's heart: it leads directly through his stomach! This dish is one of Wayne's favorites. It's a real treat, and one the man in your life is sure to savor.

Be sure to serve this dish as soon as it is ready: you wait for the biscuits and gravy, they don't wait for you.

Biscuits:
2 cups flour, plus more for dusting
1 tablespoon baking powder
1 teaspoon salt
¼ teaspoon baking soda
½ cup (1 stick) cold butter, cubed
1 cup buttermilk

Gravy:
8 ounces loose pork sausage
2 tablespoons butter
¼ cup flour
3 cups milk
½ teaspoon pepper
¼ teaspoon salt

The best biscuits require the gentlest handling. Carefully pat these out before cutting. Don't roll!

Preheat the oven to 450°F. Line a rimmed baking sheet with parchment paper.

Make the biscuits:

In a large bowl, whisk together the flour, baking powder, salt, and baking soda. Cut in the butter with a pastry cutter or two knives until the mixture resembles coarse meal. Stir in the buttermilk, mixing just until combined.

Turn the dough out onto a floured surface. Flour the top and gently pat the dough out until it is ½ inch thick. Using a floured 3-inch round cutter, cut out biscuits. Gently push the scraps together and cut again to yield a total of 8 biscuits. Transfer the biscuits to the prepared baking sheet, spacing them 1 inch apart.

Bake the biscuits for 10 to 12 minutes, until puffed and light golden brown. Remove the pan from the oven and place the biscuits on a wire rack.

Make the gravy:

In a large skillet, cook the sausage over medium-high heat, breaking it up with a spoon, until crumbled and browned, 8 to 10 minutes. Remove to a plate using a slotted spoon.

Add the butter to the sausage grease. When it is melted, add the flour, whisking constantly, and cook for 2 to 3 minutes.

Whisk in the milk, ½ cup at a time. Simmer for 3 to 4

minutes, whisking constantly, until thickened. Add the cooked sausage, pepper, and salt and cook for 1 to 2 more minutes, until heated through. Ladle the hot gravy over the hot biscuits and serve immediately.

TOMATO, EGG, AND PROSCIUTTO TARTS

Makes 8

These beautiful little tarts look like they took forever to make but come together in a snap. The secret? Store-bought puff pastry. You're going to look like a master chef.

Preheat the oven to 400°F. Line two rimmed baking sheets with parchment paper.

Unfold each puff pastry rectangle onto a prepared baking sheet and cut into 4 squares. Place on the baking sheets, spacing the squares at least 1 inch apart.

Use a sharp knife to score a border ¼ inch from the edges on each square. Do not cut all the way through the dough. Transfer the baking sheets to the freezer for 10 minutes.

In a medium bowl, mix together the tomatoes, olive oil, and thyme.

Make an egg wash by whisking 1 of the eggs with 1 tablespoon water in a small bowl.

Remove the baking sheets from the freezer and brush the borders of each square with the egg wash. Sprinkle the cheese evenly over each square, staying inside the border. Lay a piece of prosciutto over the cheese and place the tomatoes in a rough square just inside the border.

Bake for 18 to 20 minutes, until the pastries are golden brown and slightly puffed. Remove the baking sheets from the oven.

Carefully crack an egg into the center of each tart and sprinkle with salt and pepper. Return to the oven and bake for an additional 9 to 11 minutes, until the whites are set and the yolks are still runny.

Remove from the oven and use a large metal spatula to transfer the tarts to plates. Serve immediately.

1 (17.3-ounce) box (2 sheets) frozen puff pastry, thawed

2 cups cherry tomatoes, halved

2 teaspoons olive oil

1 teaspoon chopped fresh thyme

9 eggs

1 cup shredded Fontina or mozzarella cheese

8 thin slices prosciutto

Salt and pepper

SHEEPHERDER'S SKILLET

Serves 8

A hearty breakfast that has it all: bacon, potatoes, eggs, and cheese. The hash browns get crispy on the bottom, while the eggs are cooked just enough to be runny.

1 pound bacon, cut into 1-inch pieces

1 cup coarsely chopped onion

1 (30-ounce) package unseasoned frozen hash browns, thawed

8 eggs

½ teaspoon salt

¼ teaspoon pepper

1 cup shredded Cheddar cheese

Preheat the oven to 400°F.

In a 12-inch cast-iron skillet, cook the bacon and onion over medium heat until the bacon is crisp and the onion is translucent, 8 to 10 minutes. Stir in the hash browns and cook, stirring occasionally, for about 10 minutes, until the hash browns have warmed but are not yet crispy.

Make 8 wells in the potato mixture with the back of a spoon. Crack an egg into each hole and sprinkle the eggs with the salt and pepper.

Transfer the pan to the oven and bake for 10 minutes, or until the eggs are set. Remove the pan from the oven and sprinkle with the cheese. Let sit, uncovered, until the cheese is melted, then serve immediately.

BACON SPINACH GOUDA QUICHE

Serves 6 to 8

The combination of salty bacon, smoked Gouda, and creamy eggy filling is perfection. You can serve it for brunch, lunch, or even a light dinner. A crisp green salad would be an ideal accompaniment.

8 slices bacon, cut into 1-inch pieces

1 cup chopped frozen spinach, thawed and drained

1 (9-inch) prepared pie shell, baked

1½ cups shredded smoked Gouda cheese

4 eggs

1 cup milk

⅔ cup cream

½ teaspoon salt

½ teaspoon pepper

1 tablespoon sliced green onion or scallion tops

You can make your own piecrust, but a good-quality frozen or premade crust will do just as well.

Preheat the oven to 375°F.

Fry the bacon in a large skillet over medium-high heat until crisp, 8 to 10 minutes. Drain on paper towels.

Spread the spinach over the bottom of the pie shell. Layer the cheese evenly over the spinach. Sprinkle the bacon evenly on top.

In a large bowl, whisk together the eggs, milk, cream, salt, and pepper until well combined. Slowly pour the mixture into the pie shell. Sprinkle the green onions over the top.

Bake the quiche for about 40 minutes, until the crust is golden brown and a knife inserted 1 inch from the edge comes out clean. Let cool for at least 20 minutes on the counter to let the middle set. Serve warm or at room temperature.

DEBBIE'S APPLE BUTTER

Makes about 7 cups

We have several apple trees on our property in Port Orchard, Washington, but as much as we enjoy apples, Wayne and I can only eat so many. To make sure all those apples don't go to waste, the whole family makes apple butter. Our multiple slow cookers are plugged into nearly every kitchen outlet!

Apple butter is a wonderful opportunity to be creative by adding your own personal touch to the recipe. Here are three variations my family loves. Because who can resist salted caramel any-thing?

Packaged with a dozen Pumpkin Apple Crunch Muffins (page 18) or a loaf of Gratitude Bread (page 9), a jar makes a lovely hostess gift.

3 pounds tart apples, peeled, cored, and quartered (about 12 cups)

1½ cups granulated sugar

½ cup light brown sugar

1½ teaspoons ground cinnamon

½ teaspoon salt

Put the apples, granulated sugar, brown sugar, cinnamon, and salt in a 6-quart slow cooker. Cover and cook on high for 4 hours.

Sterilize jars and lids, or run them through the hottest cycle in the dishwasher.

When the apples are mushy and dark brown, stir with a wooden spoon to smooth the mixture out. It will still be a little chunky. If you prefer a smoother texture, whisk it. Pour the mixture into the hot jars, screw on the lids, and refrigerate.

Salted Caramel Apple Butter: After 4 hours in the slow cooker, add 20 unwrapped individual caramels and 1½ tea-spoons salt. Cover and cook for 15 more minutes, or until the caramels are melted. Stir with a wooden spoon until completely combined.

Fireball Cinnamon Whisky Apple Butter: After 4 hours, stir in ¼ cup Fireball Cinnamon Whisky.

Salted Caramel Fireball Cinnamon Whisky Apple But-ter: After 4 hours, add 20 unwrapped individual wrapped caramels and 1½ teaspoons salt. Cover and cook for 15 more minutes, or until the caramels are melted. Add ¼ cup Fireball Cinnamon Whisky and stir everything together with a wooden spoon.

The apple butter will keep for several weeks, covered tightly and refrigerated. Or it can be canned in a hot water bath.

If you have a windfall of apples, these recipes are easily doubled.

APPETIZERS AND SNACKS

It happens every afternoon—you could set your clock by it. At 3 p.m., my stomach lets me know it's time for a snack. I think it must be something left over from my kids' school days. They'd race in the door, toss their books down, and immediately head for the kitchen. I'd have a snack ready and I'd join them as they'd tell me about their day. All our children are grown now with families of their own, but those three o'clock cravings remain with me. While I claim to be a frequent eater, what I'm actually referring to is snacking: those little pick-me-ups that get me through the afternoon or a late-night craving.

In my humble opinion, "appetizers" is just a fancy word for snacks. Wayne and I aren't ones for big, fancy dinner parties, but give us a football game and we enjoy putting out the spread. It wouldn't be football without popcorn and chips and dips. There's always an overabundance and a variety of goodies. Most are finger-foods that are easy to grab as we pass by or stand up to cheer.

My favorite day for appetizers, though, is Thanksgiving. Because I serve the main meal at three in the afternoon, it's a long stretch between breakfast and dinner. I use appetizers to bridge the gap. Everyone pitches in and we always have some really tasty contributions.

Whatever the time of day, appetizers and snacks are the best.

GARLIC PIZZA KNOTS
WITH TOMATO DIPPING SAUCE

Makes 16 knots and 1½ cups sauce

Everyone in our family loves garlic. When I put a platter of these hearty treats out, they disappear quickly.

Make the tomato dipping sauce:

In a small bowl, whisk together the tomato paste, water, honey, onion powder, salt, garlic powder, marjoram, basil, oregano, red pepper flakes, and black pepper.

Make the garlic pizza knots:

Preheat the oven to 400°F. Line a rimmed baking sheet with parchment paper.

Remove the biscuits from the container. Cut each biscuit in half. Use your hands to roll each half into a 6-inch-long log.

Fold each pepperoni slice in half and place one in the middle of each log. Hold the pepperoni in place with a finger and tie the log into a simple knot. Place each knot on the prepared baking sheet.

In a small bowl, whisk together the butter, cheese, parsley, garlic powder, oregano, and salt. Using a pastry brush, brush the tops and sides of the knots with about half of the butter.

Bake for 14 to 17 minutes, until the tops of the knots are golden brown. Remove the pan from the oven and brush again with the rest of the butter.

Let the knots cool on the pan for 2 to 3 minutes, then serve warm with the tomato dipping sauce on the side.

Tomato dipping sauce:
1 (6-ounce) can tomato paste
¾ cup warm water
1 teaspoon honey
¾ teaspoon onion powder
½ teaspoon salt
¼ teaspoon garlic powder
¼ teaspoon dried marjoram
¼ teaspoon dried basil
¼ teaspoon dried oregano
⅛ teaspoon crushed red pepper flakes
⅛ teaspoon black pepper

Garlic pizza knots:
1 (8-count) tube refrigerated buttermilk biscuits
16 slices pepperoni
4 tablespoons (¼ cup) butter, at room temperature
2 tablespoons grated Parmesan cheese
1 tablespoon minced fresh parsley
¾ teaspoon garlic powder
½ teaspoon dried oregano
¼ teaspoon salt

MUSHROOM AND CARAMELIZED ONION BITES

Makes 20

Served on the side of a simple green salad or as an hors d'oeuvre, these elegant little bites are irresistible.

6 tablespoons (¾ cup) butter
3 cups sliced onions
2¾ cups sliced mushrooms
1 sheet (8 ounces) frozen puff pastry, thawed for 30 minutes
Flour, for dusting
1 egg, lightly beaten with 1 teaspoon water
⅔ cup shredded Parmesan cheese
¼ teaspoon garlic powder
½ teaspoon salt
⅛ teaspoon pepper
¼ cup minced fresh parsley

Preheat the oven to 400°F. Line two rimmed baking sheets with parchment paper. Position the oven racks in the top and bottom thirds of the oven.

In a large cast-iron skillet, melt 3 tablespoons of the butter over medium-low heat. Add the onions and cook, stirring occasionally, for 18 to 20 minutes, until they are very soft and golden. Remove the onions to a medium bowl.

Add the remaining 3 tablespoons butter to the skillet and melt over medium-high heat. Add the mushrooms and cook for 3 to 4 minutes, until softened. Add them to the bowl with the onions. Let the mixture cool slightly while you prepare the puff pastry.

Unfold the puff pastry on a floured surface. Using a pizza cutter or a sharp knife, cut it into 4 equal strips, each about 2¼ inches wide. Cut each strip into 5 equal pieces, each about 1¾ inches wide. Transfer the pastry to the prepared baking sheets, spacing the pieces at least 1 inch apart. Brush with the egg wash.

Add the cheese, garlic powder, salt, and pepper to the mushroom mixture and stir to combine. Place 1 tablespoon of the mixture in the center of each pastry.

Bake the pastries for 18 to 20 minutes, rotating the pans top to bottom halfway through, until they are puffed and golden brown. Sprinkle the parsley over all and transfer to a serving platter. Serve warm or at room temperature.

SWEET AND SALTY NUTS

Makes 4 cups

These nuts are addictive and are sure to quickly disappear at any party. They'd make a wonderful Christmas gift for a neighbor or co-worker. What a great way to show someone that they are appreciated.

What I enjoy is how versatile they are. Keep some on hand for unexpected company (or yourself!). Not only are they a satisfying snack, they add a delightful crunch to a salad. Or combine with your favorite dried fruits and mini-pretzels to make your own personal trail mix.

Preheat the oven to 350°F. Butter a rimmed baking sheet or line it with parchment paper.

In a large bowl, stir together the nuts and corn syrup. Add the granulated sugar, salt, and pepper and stir well to coat the nuts. Spread the mixture in a single layer on the baking sheet.

Bake for 23 to 27 minutes, stirring once halfway through, until the nuts are bubbling and lightly toasted. Remove from the oven, immediately sprinkle the raw sugar over the nuts, and toss to coat.

Transfer the nuts to a large piece of aluminum foil and spread into a single layer. Let cool for at least 30 minutes, then break the mixture apart into small chunks. Store at room temperature in an airtight container for up to 2 weeks, or in the freezer for up to 1 month.

Variation:

Sweet, Salty, and Spicy Nuts: Add ½ teaspoon chili powder and ¼ teaspoon cayenne pepper with the sugar, salt, and pepper.

1 tablespoon butter, at room temperature (optional)

4 cups pecans, walnuts, cashews, almonds, or peanuts, or a mixture

⅓ cup light corn syrup

½ cup granulated sugar

2½ teaspoons salt

½ teaspoon pepper

3 tablespoons raw or turbinado sugar

The spicy variation has a slight heat but is not too spicy.

SAVORY AND SWEET POPCORN

Makes 6 cups

Popcorn is my weakness. I could eat it every day of the week and never grow tired of it. We have more popcorn poppers than any single family should own. It's the butter. It's the salt. It's the variety and the flavors. Oh my, I'm getting a yearning for some right this moment by simply talking about it! There's little in life more pleasing than snuggling in a chair with our youngest grandson, Oliver, a bowl of popcorn, and a fun book to read aloud.

Plain buttered popcorn is delicious, but why not up the ante a little with these recipes? Serve them to your family on movie night, or set out bowls for your guests.

SAVORY

ITALIAN HERBED POPCORN

6 cups fresh plain air-popped popcorn

4 tablespoons (½ stick) butter, melted

¼ teaspoon dried basil

¼ teaspoon dried marjoram

¼ teaspoon dried oregano

¼ teaspoon dried rosemary

¼ teaspoon dried thyme

½ teaspoon salt

PARMESAN POPCORN

6 cups fresh plain air-popped popcorn

4 tablespoons (½ stick) butter, melted

½ cup finely shredded Parmesan cheese

¼ teaspoon salt

In a large bowl, toss the popcorn with butter until evenly coated. Toss with the spices or cheese and salt until evenly coated. Serve hot.

Line two rimmed baking sheets with parchment paper.

Pour the dark chocolate chips into a microwave-safe bowl. Microwave on high in 30-second increments until melted.

In a separate microwave-safe bowl, microwave the white chocolate chips in 30-second increments until melted.

In a large bowl, toss the hot popcorn with the coconut oil and ¼ teaspoon of the salt. Divide evenly between the baking sheets, spreading the popcorn out into a single layer.

Dip a spoon into the dark chocolate and drizzle it all over the popcorn. Place the baking sheets in the refrigerator for 5 minutes to set the chocolate.

Remove the baking sheets from the refrigerator and drizzle the popcorn with the white chocolate. Sprinkle with the remaining ⅛ teaspoon salt. Place in the refrigerator for 10 minutes to set.

Remove from the refrigerator and break the popcorn into chunks.

Line two rimmed baking sheets with parchment paper.

In a large bowl, toss the popcorn with the coconut oil and ¼ teaspoon of the salt. Divide between the two baking sheets, spreading the popcorn into a single layer.

In a small saucepan, heat the caramels with the water over medium heat, stirring often, until melted and smooth, 4 to 5 minutes. Remove the pan from the heat and stir in the remaining ½ teaspoon salt.

Dip a spoon into the hot caramel and drizzle it all over the popcorn. Enjoy immediately while still gooey, or wait a few minutes until the caramel has hardened.

SWEET

WHITE AND DARK CHOCOLATE–DRIZZLED POPCORN

¼ cup dark chocolate chips

¼ cup white chocolate chips

6 cups fresh plain air-popped popcorn

2 teaspoons coconut oil, melted

⅜ teaspoon salt

SALTED CARAMEL–DRIZZLED POPCORN

6 cups fresh plain air-popped popcorn

2 teaspoons coconut oil, melted

¾ teaspoon salt

20 caramel squares, such as Kraft, unwrapped

2 tablespoons water

All of these variations make fun party favors or gifts. Let the sweet versions cool before you pack them up, and keep them cool. They will keep in an airtight container at room temperature for 2 to 3 days.

TOMATILLO SALSA

Makes 5 cups

I grow tomatillos every year specifically for this salsa. It's become a family staple and is good on just about anything. The plants are carefully tended by Melina Heath, who works wonders with my entire yard.

2 or 3 tomatillos, husks removed and rinsed

2 jalapeño chiles, stems removed

1 or 2 serrano chiles, stems removed

4 garlic cloves, peeled

1½ teaspoons salt

1 cup tightly packed fresh cilantro leaves

1 bunch green onions or scallions, coarsely chopped

1 (28-ounce) can whole tomatoes in juice

1 teaspoon lime juice

Bring a large pot of water to a boil over medium-high heat. Add the tomatillos, jalapeños, 1 of the serranos, and the garlic, then boil, uncovered, for 7 to 10 minutes, until the tomatillos begin to turn brown and the chiles are tender when pierced with a knife. Remove from the heat and cool for 15 minutes.

Transfer the tomatillos, jalapeños, serrano, garlic, and ¼ cup of the cooking water to a food processor. Add the salt, cilantro, green onions, tomatoes and their juice, and lime juice. Pulse until blended into a puree with a little texture. Taste, then add the remaining boiled serrano if you'd like more heat, and pulse until combined.

Transfer the salsa to a serving bowl, cover with plastic wrap, and refrigerate until cool. Serve with tortilla chips.

BACON-WRAPPED DATES

Makes 16

Anything that's sweet and salty calls my name. I serve these with drinks or wine before dinner, or as a garnish to a simple green salad.

Preheat the oven to 375°F. Line a rimmed baking sheet with aluminum foil.

Lay out a piece of bacon. Place a date at one end and roll it up in the bacon strip. Secure the bacon with a toothpick. Place the date on the prepared baking sheet.

Repeat with remaining dates and bacon.

Bake for 25 to 30 minutes, until the bacon is crisp. Remove from the baking sheet and serve warm or at room temperature.

16 slices bacon
16 pitted dates

WARM GOAT CHEESE
AND ROASTED CHERRY TOMATO DIP

Serves 4 to 6

My garden is filled with a variety of tomato plants and sweet, bite-size cherry tomatoes are my favorites.

Okay, confession time: half of them get eaten before they ever make it to the kitchen. There's little more satisfying than to pick them fresh off the vine, warmed from the sun, and enjoy them standing in the middle of the garden.

Preheat the oven to 350°F.

In a medium bowl, mix together the cheese, garlic, 2 tablespoons of the olive oil, the salt, lemon zest, lemon juice, and parsley.

Break the goat cheese into large chunks, add to the bowl, and mix until well incorporated.

Spread half of the cheese mixture in a pie plate or other shallow baking dish. Strew half of the tomatoes evenly over the cheese and spread the rest of the cheese mixture evenly on top.

Distribute the remaining tomatoes on top and drizzle with the remaining 1 tablespoon olive oil.

Bake for 30 to 35 minutes, until the cheese is hot and the tomatoes are slightly blistered.

Remove the pan from the oven and let cool for 5 minutes. Serve with crackers or toasted baguette slices.

1 cup whole-milk ricotta cheese

¾ teaspoon minced garlic

3 tablespoons olive oil

½ teaspoon salt

Zest of 1 lemon

2 teaspoons lemon juice

¼ cup chopped fresh parsley

1 (8-ounce) log goat cheese

2½ cups cherry tomatoes

Crackers or toasted baguette slices, for serving

HUMMUS

Makes 1½ cups

I am especially fond of hummus. And really, what's not to like? It's low-calorie, tasty, and easy to make. I've included a few of my favorite variations, but get creative and make up a few of your own.

¼ cup well-stirred tahini

¼ cup lemon juice

¾ teaspoon minced garlic

2 tablespoons extra virgin olive oil, plus more for serving

¾ teaspoon salt

½ teaspoon ground cumin, or to taste

1 (15-ounce) can chickpeas (garbanzo beans), drained and rinsed well

2 tablespoons water, plus more if needed

⅛ teaspoon paprika, for garnish

Tahini can be found with the nut butters in your grocery store; a jar will make multiple batches of hummus.

In a food processor, process the tahini and lemon juice for 1 minute. Scrape down the sides and bottom of the bowl and process for another minute, or until much lighter in color.

Add the garlic, olive oil, salt, cumin, and half of the chickpeas and process for 1 minute. Scrape down the bowl well.

Add the rest of the chickpeas and the water and process for another 2 minutes. If your hummus is still very thick, add a little more water, 1 tablespoon at a time, and process until it reaches your desired consistency.

Transfer the hummus to a serving bowl. Drizzle with a little oil and sprinkle the paprika on top.

Roasted Red Pepper Hummus: Add ¾ cup drained chopped, jarred roasted red peppers with the first half of the chickpeas. You may not need to add additional water with the second half of the chickpeas. Garnish with 2 tablespoons drained chopped, jarred roasted red peppers instead of paprika.

Roasted Garlic Hummus: Substitute 1 head of roasted garlic cloves (about ¼ cup) for the fresh garlic. See page 5 for instructions on roasting garlic.

Kalamata Olive Hummus: Add ½ cup pitted Kalamata olives with the first half of the chickpeas. Reduce the salt to ½ teaspoon. Garnish with 2 tablespoons chopped Kalamata olives instead of paprika.

SEVEN-LAYER DIP

Serves 10

I've seen several variations of seven-layer dip over the years. It's a perfect dip for a party, game, or potluck served with chips and assorted veggies like carrot sticks, thickly sliced radishes, bell pepper spears, and cucumber spears.

In a medium bowl, mix together the beans, canned tomatoes and green chiles, chili powder, ¾ teaspoon of the cumin, ¼ teaspoon of the garlic powder, ½ teaspoon of the salt, and the pepper. Spread evenly in a 7 x 11-inch serving dish.

Halve the avocados, remove the pits, and scoop the flesh into a medium bowl. Mash with a fork until creamy, then add the lime juice, the remaining ¼ teaspoon cumin, ¼ teaspoon garlic powder, and ¼ teaspoon salt. Set aside 2 tablespoons of the cilantro and add the rest to the bowl. Stir until combined. Spread evenly on top of the bean layer.

Spread the sour cream evenly on top of the avocado layer, then sprinkle the cheeses evenly over the top. Layer on the olives, then the fresh tomatoes, green onions, and the reserved cilantro on top. Serve immediately, or cover tightly and refrigerate for up to 1 day.

1 (16-ounce) can refried beans

1 (16-ounce) can diced tomatoes and green chiles, drained

1 tablespoon chili powder

1 teaspoon ground cumin

½ teaspoon garlic powder

¾ teaspoon salt

¼ teaspoon pepper

3 medium avocados

1 tablespoon lime juice

½ cup chopped fresh cilantro

1 cup sour cream

1 cup shredded Cheddar cheese

1 cup shredded Monterey Jack cheese

1 (6-ounce) can sliced black olives, drained

3 Roma tomatoes, diced

⅓ cup sliced green onions or scallions

This recipe calls for homemade guacamole, but 2½ cups of store-bought guacamole can be used if you want a shortcut.

SOUPS AND SALADS

There's nothing Wayne and I enjoy more than a hot bowl of soup on a windy, rainy day. We have an abundance of these types of days here in the Pacific Northwest, although to be fair, Seattle gets less rainfall than New York City, if you can believe it! (We do, however, have more rainy days because a lot of our moisture comes in the form of drizzle.)

Our oldest daughter, Jody, is the soup queen in our family. She could write her own cookbook on the number of wonderful soup recipes she's shared over the years. And when I introduced cooking to the grandkids, I started them off with an easy soup recipe because it made enough for them to take home and share with their families.

Years ago, when most of the grandkids at the time were around eight and nine years old, I started Grandma Camp with our three granddaughters, setting aside one week each summer. Each year I shared my passions with them. I gave the girls a journal to write in each morning, taught them to knit, and let them look through my large collection of cookbooks. They'd each choose a dish they wanted to prepare, and then we'd head to the kitchen. That week has become an annual tradition in our family. One year the girls and I drove to Yakima, where I grew up, and I shared story upon story of my childhood days. They *loved* it. Grandpa Camp evolved from this, and because we have eight grandsons, Wayne requires help from our son, Ted. He cheated and took them on cruises and other short vacations. Still, it's a special time for all of our grandchildren, and that's what matters.

SOUPS

CARROT GINGER SOUP

Serves 4 to 6

Here's a colorful soup you can serve all year long: it's delicious hot, room temperature, or even cold. Pair it with Debbie's Grandkids' Rolls (page 125) for a light lunch.

In a medium saucepan, melt the butter over medium-high heat. Add the onion and cook until translucent, 5 to 7 minutes.

Add the carrots, ginger, and chicken broth to the pan and bring to a boil. Cover, turn the heat down to low, and simmer for about 10 minutes, until the carrots are tender.

Puree the soup with an immersion blender until very smooth. Alternatively, puree the soup in batches in a standing blender. Season with salt and pepper, ladle into bowls, and serve.

2 tablespoons unsalted butter
½ cup chopped onion
4 cups sliced carrots
2 tablespoons chopped fresh ginger
4 cups chicken broth
Salt and pepper

It will keep, covered, for up to 3 days in the refrigerator, and for up to 3 months frozen.

SAUSAGE, KALE, AND POTATO SOUP

Serves 4 to 6

I confess I'm not a big fan of kale, but I have no complaints when I add it to this soup. It really is delicious and the perfect complement. You may be surprised that something so tasty can be made with so few simple ingredients and in less than a half hour. It's a dish Cassie Carter from Last One Home *would cook for herself and her daughter, Amiee.*

In a large saucepan, brown the sausage over medium heat, 8 to 10 minutes.

Add the onion and cook until soft and translucent, about 5 minutes. Add the garlic and cook for 1 minute. Add the potatoes, red pepper flakes, chicken broth, and water. Bring to a boil, then reduce the heat to medium, cover, and cook until the potatoes are fork tender, about 5 minutes.

Stir in the kale and half-and-half. Increase the heat, bring to a low boil, and cook for 3 more minutes, until the kale is wilted. Season with salt and pepper to taste. Ladle into bowls and serve hot.

1 pound ground sweet Italian sausage

1 cup diced onion

1 teaspoon minced garlic

4 cups (½-inch) cubed red potatoes

¼ teaspoon crushed red pepper flakes

3½ cups chicken broth

1 cup water

1 bunch kale, washed, stems removed and coarsely chopped

⅓ cup half-and-half

Salt and pepper

If you can only find sausage links, just remove the meat from the casings.

This will keep, covered, in the refrigerator for up to 3 days and can be frozen for up to 3 months.

DEBBIE'S MOM'S BORSCHT

Serves 8 to 10

This meaty soup was a staple in the Adler family. The minute my mom knew my grandpa was coming to dinner, she'd put on a huge pot of this soup; it was his favorite. When I make it for my family, it brings back a multitude of childhood memories.

2 to 3 pounds bone-in chuck roast

12 cups water

1 tablespoon plus 1 teaspoon salt

2 tablespoons vegetable oil

1 cup diced onion

3 cups shredded beets (about 3 medium)

1 cup grated carrots

1 tablespoon white or cider vinegar

1 tablespoon sugar

2 cups (½-inch) cubed russet potatoes

4 cups shredded green cabbage

1 (14.5-ounce) can diced tomatoes

1½ teaspoons minced garlic

1 bay leaf

¼ teaspoon pepper

Sour cream, for garnish

This will keep covered in the refrigerator for up to 3 days and frozen for up to 3 months.

Place the beef in a large saucepan and add the water and 1 tablespoon of the salt. Bring to a boil over medium-high heat, then cover and reduce the heat to medium-low. Simmer for 5 minutes, then uncover and skim off the foam. Cover again and simmer for 40 minutes.

Heat the oil in a large skillet over medium-high heat until shimmering. Add the onion and cook for 3 to 4 minutes, until it is translucent and soft. Add the beets and carrots and cook for 5 minutes, stirring occasionally. Reduce the heat to medium-low and add the vinegar and sugar. Cook for 4 to 5 more minutes, stirring occasionally, until very soft and all the liquid has evaporated.

After the meat has cooked for 45 minutes total, remove it with tongs to a cutting board and cut it into 1-inch cubes. Discard the bone.

Add the meat back to the pot. Add the beet mixture, potatoes, cabbage, diced tomatoes with their juice, garlic, bay leaf, pepper, and the remaining 1 teaspoon salt. Bring to a boil, then reduce the heat, cover, and simmer for 15 to 20 minutes, until the potatoes are fork tender and the cabbage is very soft.

Ladle into bowls and serve hot, topped with a dollop of sour cream.

DEBBIE'S LIGHT CLAM CHOWDER

Serves 8 to 10

My husband, Wayne, likes to add soda crackers to his soup. I make a lighter version of the traditional chowder so when he crumbles crackers on top it doesn't get too thick.

Wayne and I are fortunate enough to own waterfront property on Hood Canal. Digging up clams on our beach is great fun for all of the family; my grandson James is a clam-digging master. If you can't dig your own clams, fresh from the fishmonger, frozen, or canned clams will work just as well.

In a large saucepan, cook the bacon, onion, and celery over medium-high heat until the bacon is slightly crisp and the vegetables are soft, about 10 minutes. Add the chicken broth and potatoes and bring to a boil, scraping the bottom to loosen any browned bits. Reduce the heat to low, cover, and simmer for 8 to 10 minutes, until the potatoes are fork tender.

In a separate bowl, whisk the flour into ½ cup of the evaporated milk, then stir into the soup. Stir in the remaining 1 cup evaporated milk and all of the clams and juice. Raise the heat to medium and bring to a boil. Reduce the heat and simmer, uncovered, for 5 to 7 minutes, until the clams are cooked and the soup has thickened. Ladle into bowls and serve hot.

4 slices bacon, cut into ½-inch slices

1 cup chopped onion

¾ cup chopped celery

4 cups chicken broth

3 cups (½-inch) cubed russet potatoes

¼ cup Wondra flour

1½ cups evaporated milk

2 (6.5-ounce) cans chopped clams in juice

BACON CORN CHOWDER

Serves 4 to 6

Chowder doesn't have to have clams. Bacon adds a smoky flavor that complements the sweet corn in this rich soup.

2 (15.25-ounce) cans corn, drained

3 cups chicken broth

6 slices bacon, chopped

½ cup diced onion

1¾ cups (½-inch) cubed red potatoes

¼ teaspoon salt

¼ teaspoon pepper

½ cup cream

2 tablespoons chopped fresh chives

Pour 1 can of corn and 1 cup of chicken broth into the blender and blend until very smooth.

In a large, heavy-bottomed saucepan, cook the bacon over medium heat until crisp, 8 to 10 minutes. Remove the bacon and drain on paper towels.

Pour out all but 1 tablespoon of the bacon fat. Fry the onion in the remaining fat over medium-high heat until soft, about 5 minutes. Add the potatoes, salt, pepper, the remaining can of corn, and the remaining 2 cups chicken broth. Bring to a boil, then reduce the heat to medium and simmer until the potatoes are tender, about 15 minutes. Stir in the cream and cooked bacon. Ladle into bowls and serve hot, garnished with the chives.

CHEESEBURGER SOUP

Serves 8 to 10

Anything with cheese will thrill the kids and the men in your life. A bowl of this on a cold, wet day will warm you down to your toes.

In a large saucepan, cook the beef over medium-high heat, stirring to break it up, until no longer pink, 8 to 10 minutes. Drain and discard the fat. Remove the beef to a bowl.

In the same pan, melt 1 tablespoon of the butter. Add the onion and celery and cook until the onion is soft and translucent, about 5 minutes. Add the potatoes, beef broth, tomatoes, parsley, and the cooked beef. Bring to a boil, then cover and reduce the heat to low. Simmer until the potatoes are tender, 12 to 15 minutes.

In a small saucepan, melt the remaining 3 tablespoons butter over medium heat. Whisk in the flour and cook, stirring constantly, for 3 to 5 minutes, until bubbly. Stir the mixture into the soup and bring to a boil. Cook for 2 to 3 minutes. Add the cheese, milk, salt, and pepper. Stir until the cheese is melted.

Ladle into bowls and serve hot, topped with a dollop of sour cream.

1 pound ground beef

4 tablespoons (½ stick) butter

1 cup chopped onion

1½ cups diced celery

4 cups (½-inch) cubed red potatoes

2 (14.5-ounce) cans low-sodium beef broth

1 (14.5-ounce) can diced tomatoes

2 teaspoons parsley flakes

¼ cup flour

1 (16-ounce) package Velveeta, cubed

1½ cups milk

¾ teaspoon salt

½ teaspoon pepper

Sour cream, for garnish

DRIED SOUP MIXES

These soup mixes make great housewarming, hostess, or Christmas gifts. You might want to keep a couple in the pantry, too!

I'll admit I'm not a big fan of lentils, but friends tell me I'm in the minority. They're so good for you, and the Rainbow Lentil Soup comes together in less than an hour, so I had to include it.

TACO SOUP

Serves 6 to 8

In a pint mason jar, layer the red beans, black beans, pinto beans, barley, vegetable blend, and dried onion. Pour the packet of taco seasoning and salt into a small zip-top bag or square of plastic wrap. Squeeze out all the air, seal, and place in the jar. Place the lid and ring on top and screw closed. Attach the cooking directions.

Cooking directions:

Remove the seasonings and pour the contents of the jar into a large saucepan. Add 6 cups water. Cover and bring to a boil over high heat. Remove from the heat and let sit, covered, for 1 hour.

Add the seasonings, one 14-ounce can diced tomatoes, and 2 cups chicken broth. Cover and bring to a boil. Reduce the heat to medium-low and simmer for 60 to 80 minutes, until the beans are tender. Stir in 2 cups diced cooked chicken, if desired, and warm through. Serve with shredded Cheddar cheese and sour cream.

½ cup dried red beans

¼ cup dried black beans

¼ cup dried pinto beans

2 tablespoons pearl barley

½ cup dried vegetable blend

1 tablespoon dried minced onion

1 packet taco seasoning

1 teaspoon salt

RAINBOW LENTIL SOUP

Serves 6 to 8

½ cup white rice
¼ cup red lentils
¼ cup brown lentils
¼ cup green lentils
¼ cup yellow lentils
¼ cup dried vegetable blend
2 teaspoons dried minced onion
1 bay leaf
¾ teaspoon dried parsley
¼ teaspoon garlic powder
¼ teaspoon dried basil
¼ teaspoon dried oregano
⅛ teaspoon dried thyme

In a pint mason jar, layer the rice, red lentils, brown lentils, green lentils, yellow lentils, vegetable blend, and dried onion. In a small zip-top plastic bag or on a square of plastic wrap, layer the bay leaf, parsley, garlic powder, basil, oregano, and thyme. Squeeze out all the air, seal, and place in the jar. Place the lid and ring on top and screw closed. Attach the cooking directions.

Cooking directions:

Dump the spices and the contents of the jar into a large pot. Add 3 cups chicken broth and 4 cups water; bring to a boil over high heat. Cover, reduce the heat to low, and simmer, stirring occasionally, for 45 to 55 minutes, until the rice and lentils are tender. Discard the bay leaf and stir in 2 cups cubed ham, if desired. Season with salt and pepper. Add more water if the soup is too thick.

SPICY BLACK BEAN SOUP

Serves 6 to 8

This isn't too spicy, so if you know someone who likes it hot, consider attaching a mini bottle of hot sauce along with the cooking directions. I enjoy spicy food. Wayne tells me food shouldn't hurt, but I can't resist.

1½ cups dried black beans
¼ cup dried navy beans
1 tablespoon dried onion flakes
1 tablespoon ground cumin
2 teaspoons chili powder
1 teaspoon garlic powder
½ teaspoon salt
¼ teaspoon black pepper
⅛ teaspoon crushed red pepper flakes
1 bay leaf

In a pint mason jar, layer one-third of the black beans, then half of the navy beans. Repeat the layers. In a small zip-top bag or on a square of plastic wrap, layer the dried onion, cumin, chili powder, garlic powder, salt, black pepper, red pepper flakes, and bay leaf. Squeeze out all the air, seal, and place in the jar. Place the lid and ring on top and screw closed. Attach the cooking directions.

Cooking directions:

Dump the spices and beans into a large saucepan. Add 6 cups water or vegetable broth and bring to a boil over high heat. Cover, reduce the heat to low, and simmer, stirring occasionally, for 1½ to 2 hours, until the beans are tender. Serve topped with sour cream.

Other topping ideas: shredded Monterey Jack cheese, chopped cilantro, minced jalapeño.

SALADS

KALE CAESAR SALAD

Serves 4

I said earlier that I wasn't a fan of kale, but substituting antioxidant-rich kale for romaine lettuce in this recipe is a great way to add extra vitamins and nutrients to your diet. Discard the bigger ribs of kale, but the finer ones add a great crunch. The creamy, salty dressing is the star here, so your family might not even notice the swap!

This salad is best if you don't overdress it. Better to use less when you toss it, and let everyone add more to her or his taste.

Dressing:
1 cup mayonnaise
1½ teaspoons minced garlic
2 tablespoons lemon juice
1 teaspoon Dijon mustard
1 teaspoon Worcestershire sauce
1 teaspoon anchovy paste
¼ teaspoon salt
¼ teaspoon pepper
½ cup freshly grated Parmesan cheese

Salad:
8 cups washed and torn kale leaves, fine stems included
1 cup shaved Parmesan cheese

Make the dressing:

In a small bowl, whisk together the mayonnaise, garlic, lemon juice, mustard, Worcestershire sauce, anchovy paste, salt, and pepper. Stir in the grated cheese.

Make the salad:

In a large bowl, toss the kale with ½ cup of the dressing. Let it sit for 5 minutes. Add the shaved cheese and toss again, adding more dressing if desired. Serve with the remaining dressing.

WATERMELON FETA SALAD WITH BALSAMIC REDUCTION

Serves 6 to 8

Here we go with sweet and salty again! It's a perfect balance of sweet, fresh watermelon with salty feta and tangy-sweet balsamic reduction, and the watermelon makes this so fresh and appealing to the eye. Serve this at your next BBQ!

Make the balsamic reduction:

In a medium saucepan, combine the vinegar and honey over medium heat. Bring to a boil, then reduce the heat to medium-low and simmer for 12 to 15 minutes, stirring frequently, until the mixture is syrupy and has reduced to ½ cup. Be careful not to reduce beyond ½ cup or it will start to burn. Remove from the heat and let cool completely. It will thicken more as it cools.

Make the salad:

Arrange the watermelon on a big platter and sprinkle the cheese evenly over the top. Drizzle on the balsamic reduction, or serve it in a serving pitcher alongside so people can serve themselves.

Balsamic reduction:
1 cup balsamic vinegar
⅓ cup honey

Salad:
8 cups cubed seedless watermelon
1 cup crumbled feta cheese

If you can't find seedless watermelon, seed your melon before you cut it into cubes.

BROCCOLI APPLE CHEDDAR SALAD

Serves 8 to 10, or more if it's part of a buffet

I grew up in Yakima, Washington, also known as the Apple Capital of the World (although this is a title that is hotly contested by Wenatchee, Washington). I ate a lot of apples growing up, and I still enjoy them to this day.

You'll find this salad to be a great complement to any meal, or even a meal by itself. In Love Letters, *from the Rose Harbor Inn series, Maggie and Roy came from Yakima to stay at the inn. I'm sure they brought Jo Marie a box of apples.*

Make the dressing:

In a small bowl, whisk together the mayonnaise, vinegar, and sugar until well blended. Stir in the poppy seeds. Cover and refrigerate until ready to use.

Fill a large bowl with ice water.

Prepare the broccoli:

Bring a large pot of water to a boil. Add the broccoli and cook for 30 seconds. Drain the broccoli and immediately place it in the ice water. Let it cool in the water for at least 5 minutes. Drain well, lay on paper towels or a dish towel, and cover with another paper towel or dish towel.

Assemble the salad:

In a large bowl, combine the apple, cheese, cranberries, sunflower seeds, and almonds. Add the broccoli. Pour in the dressing and mix gently until well combined. Refrigerate until ready to serve.

Dressing:
1 cup mayonnaise

2 tablespoons apple cider vinegar

2 tablespoons plus 2 teaspoons sugar

1 teaspoon poppy seeds

Salad:
8 cups broccoli florets

1 cup chopped unpeeled apple

8 ounces sharp Cheddar cheese, cut into ½-inch cubes

¾ cup dried cranberries

½ cup sunflower seeds

¾ cup sliced almonds

CRUNCHY RAMEN SALAD
WITH HONEY-GINGER VINAIGRETTE

Serves 8

Who knew there were so many inventive ways to use ramen noodles? It's the medley of sweet, salty, crispy, and tangy that makes this dish. Everyone in the family enjoys this special salad.

Crunchy ramen:
2 packages ramen noodles, seasoning packets discarded
½ cup sliced almonds

Dressing:
½ cup vegetable oil
¼ cup honey
⅓ cup rice vinegar
1 tablespoon grated fresh ginger
4 teaspoons soy sauce
2 teaspoons toasted sesame oil

Salad:
2 cups shredded green cabbage
2 cups shredded red cabbage
2 cups halved mandarin orange slices
1 cup shredded carrots
1 cup shelled edamame, cooked and cooled
½ cup sliced green onions or scallions
2 tablespoons sesame seeds

Make the crunchy ramen:

Preheat the oven to 400°F. Line a rimmed baking sheet with aluminum foil.

Break the ramen noodles into chunks on the baking sheet. Stir in the almonds and shake the pan to spread everything into an even layer.

Bake for 5 to 8 minutes, stirring halfway through, until the noodles and almonds are golden brown. Remove from the oven and let cool on the baking sheet.

Make the dressing:

In a medium bowl, whisk together the vegetable oil, honey, rice vinegar, ginger, soy sauce, and sesame oil.

Assemble the salad:

In a large bowl, mix together the red and green cabbage, mandarin oranges, carrots, edamame, green onions, sesame seeds, and toasted noodles and almonds. Pour the dressing over the salad and toss to combine. Serve immediately.

You can make the crunchy ramen and dressing the day before. Store the ramen in an airtight container at room temperature and the dressing in a covered jar in the refrigerator.

MAINS

A couple years after I was first published, *Newsweek* magazine did an interview with me. I was mailed an advance copy that featured the article with my photograph. Ted was the first one home from school the day it arrived, and I nearly tackled him in my eagerness to show him the magazine, convinced he'd be as excited as I was. He glanced at it, then looked up and said, "That's great, Mom, but are my gym shorts washed?" Ah, such is the life of the famous author. To my husband and children, I've always been the wife and the mother, and really, that has always been the most important role in my life.

I was a mother to our children first and foremost, after being a wife, and that meant all the normal things a mother does: taking the kids to dentist appointments, soccer practices, after-school activities, church, Scouts, music lessons, and the list goes on.

And dinner: the highlight of the day, preparing and serving dinner to my family. After a long day on a construction site, Wayne knew that when he arrived home, dinner would be ready. We all looked forward to sharing this meal together whenever possible.

This section of the recipe book is called Mains, and while it refers to the *main course* of the meal, to me, it also means the *main part* of the life of a family—the gathering together to share the events of the day, to laugh, to complain, to listen, and to be a part of a whole. I'm grateful Wayne and I could create this tradition of gathering for dinner with our children, and it has paid the richest of dividends with their families now.

GRILLED FISH TACOS
WITH CILANTRO-LIME SAUCE

Serves 6 to 8

Fish tacos are my absolute favorite. I made certain this recipe was included in the cookbook for that very reason. I can picture Nichole and Rocco from A Girl's Guide to Moving On *enjoying these tacos on a Friday night date.*

Make the sauce:

In a blender or food processor, blend the cilantro and lime juice until the cilantro is finely chopped. Add the mayonnaise and sour cream and blend until smooth. Pour into a bowl, cover, and refrigerate until ready to serve.

Make the fish:

In a shallow baking dish, whisk together the vegetable oil, lime juice, garlic powder, cumin, and chili powder. Pat the fish dry, then place it in the baking dish. Turn the fish in the marinade until coated. Cover and refrigerate for 15 minutes or up to 2 hours.

Heat an outdoor grill over medium-high heat until hot. Use tongs to dip a paper towel in oil, then brush on the grate. Place the fish on the grill and cook for 3 to 4 minutes per side, until flaky. Use a large metal spatula to remove the fish from the grill to a serving dish. Use a fork to gently break up the fish into chunks.

To serve, take a warm corn tortilla and fill it with a few pieces of fish, cabbage, a squeeze of lime, and a drizzle of sauce over the top.

Cilantro-lime sauce:
1 cup packed fresh cilantro leaves
3 tablespoons lime juice
½ cup mayonnaise
½ cup sour cream

Fish:
¼ cup vegetable oil
2 tablespoons lime juice
½ teaspoon garlic powder
½ teaspoon ground cumin
½ teaspoon chili powder
2 pounds cod fillets

Corn tortillas, warmed, for serving
2 cups shredded cabbage, for serving
Lime wedges, for serving

You can use any firm-fleshed white fish if you can't get or don't like cod. The creamy sauce can be made a day ahead and stored, covered, in the refrigerator.

If grilling outdoors isn't an option, you can cook the fish on a ridged grill pan on your stovetop.

GARLIC SALMON PASTA
IN A SPICY CREAM SAUCE

Serves 4 to 6

The Pacific Northwest is famous for its salmon. Our grandson Isaiah is the salmon lover in our family. He has been known to catch his own. This dish of pasta and salmon in a creamy cheesy sauce puts a new spin on an old favorite.

8 ounces fettuccine noodles

8 ounces salmon fillet

⅛ teaspoon salt

⅛ teaspoon black pepper

2 tablespoons vegetable or olive oil

2 tablespoons butter

1 tablespoon minced garlic

⅛ teaspoon crushed red pepper flakes

1½ cups half-and-half

1½ cups finely grated Parmesan cheese

2 teaspoons paprika

¼ teaspoon salt

⅓ cup chopped fresh parsley

Cook the fettuccine according to the package directions to al dente. Drain and set aside.

Season the flesh side of the salmon fillet with the salt and pepper.

In a 12-inch skillet, heat the oil over medium-high heat until shimmering. Place the salmon fillet in the pan, skin-side down, and cook for 5 minutes. Flip the salmon over and cook for 1 more minute, until the fish just turns opaque all the way through. Remove the salmon to a plate and remove the skin. Cut the salmon into bite-size cubes.

In the same pan, melt the butter over medium heat. Add the garlic and red pepper flakes and cook for 1 minute, or until the garlic is fragrant. Whisk in the half-and-half and bring to a simmer, whisking constantly. Add the cheese, paprika, and salt and whisk until the cheese is melted. Add the fettuccine to the pan and toss with the sauce. Add the salmon cubes and toss until coated with the sauce and heated through. Add the parsley, toss the pasta 2 or 3 times, and serve immediately.

SLOW COOKER HONEY GARLIC CHICKEN

Serves 4 to 6

You're going to lick your fingers clean on this sweet, savory, and sticky chicken dish. It tastes like you spent hours in the kitchen, but it couldn't be easier to prepare. Serve it with white or brown rice and a steamed green vegetable.

Place the chicken thighs in the bottom of a 6-quart slow cooker.

In a small bowl, whisk together the soy sauce, honey, garlic, and red pepper flakes. Pour the mixture all over the chicken. Cover and cook on high for 3 hours or low for 6 hours.

Remove the chicken to an aluminum foil– or parchment paper–lined rimmed baking sheet. Leave the sauce in the slow cooker. Position the oven rack as close to the heating element as possible and preheat the broiler.

Whisk together the water and cornstarch to make a slurry. Stir it into the sauce, and let cook for 2 to 3 minutes, uncovered, until thickened.

Broil the chicken for 2 to 3 minutes, until the skin just begins to crisp and char.

Transfer the chicken to a serving platter and sprinkle with the green onions and sesame seeds. Pour the sauce into a serving pitcher or bowl and serve.

8 bone-in skin-on chicken thighs
½ cup soy sauce
⅓ cup honey
1½ tablespoons minced garlic
¼ teaspoon crushed red pepper flakes
¼ cup water
2 tablespoons cornstarch
¼ cup sliced green onion or scallion tops
2 tablespoons sesame seeds

CURRIED CHICKEN SALAD

Serves 4

Wayne and I own The Grey House Café in Port Orchard, Washington, which is known for this curried chicken salad. The café serves it on homemade cottage bread, which is just the type of bread Nikolai from A Girl's Guide to Moving On *would bake for Leanne.*

½ cup mayonnaise
¾ teaspoon curry powder
⅛ teaspoon salt
½ cup diced celery
⅓ cup raisins
1½ cups diced apple
1½ cups cubed cooked chicken

In a large bowl, whisk together the mayonnaise, curry powder, and salt. Add the celery, raisins, and apple and mix well. Gently fold in the chicken. Cover and refrigerate for at least 1 hour before serving.

SOUTHWEST BBQ CHICKEN SALAD

Serves 6 to 8

Boldly seasoned but not too spicy, this main-dish salad is light but still satisfying.

Dressing:
1 cup mayonnaise
¾ cup milk
1½ teaspoons chili powder
¾ teaspoon garlic powder
¾ teaspoon sugar
½ teaspoon onion powder
½ teaspoon ground cumin

Chicken:
½ teaspoon salt
¼ teaspoon pepper
2 pounds boneless, skinless chicken breasts
½ cup barbecue sauce

Salad:
1 head romaine lettuce, torn into bite-size pieces
2 red bell peppers, seeded and sliced into thin strips
1 (15.25-ounce) can corn, drained
1 (2.25-ounce) can sliced black olives, drained
1 cup halved grape tomatoes
½ cup shredded Cheddar cheese
½ cup shredded Monterey Jack cheese
2 cups crispy tortilla strips or crushed tortilla chips

Make the dressing:

In a medium bowl, whisk together the mayonnaise, milk, chili powder, garlic powder, sugar, onion powder, and cumin. Cover and refrigerate until ready to use.

Make the chicken:

Prepare a grill or preheat the broiler.

Sprinkle the salt and pepper on both sides of the chicken breasts. Brush with the barbecue sauce.

Grill or broil for 5 minutes, then flip and cook for 4 to 8 minutes on the other side, depending on the thickness of the chicken breast, until an instant-read thermometer reads 165°F. Remove the chicken to a plate and let stand for 5 minutes, then slice into ½-inch strips.

Assemble the salad:

In a large bowl, toss the lettuce with the bell peppers, corn, olives, tomatoes, and cheeses. Divide the salad among six to eight plates and top with the sliced chicken. Sprinkle with the tortilla strips or crushed chips and serve.

Use your favorite barbecue sauce, homemade or store-bought. You can make the chicken on an indoor or outdoor grill, or under the broiler.

LACOMBE'S SPARE RIB SPAGHETTI

Serves 6 to 8

Our daughter Adele was given this recipe from her mother-in-law, Char LaCombe, to cook for her husband, Kevin. It has since become a Macomber family favorite. It can be cooked in a slow cooker (see variation below), and it's one of those time-tested recipes that never fails to delight.

Heat the oil in large saucepan over medium-high heat until shimmering. Add the onion and cook until translucent and soft, 6 to 8 minutes.

Add the crushed tomatoes, beef broth, tomato paste, garlic, parsley, Italian seasoning, oregano, basil, salt, and pepper. Cover and bring to a boil, then reduce the heat to a simmer.

Preheat the broiler. Line a rimmed baking sheet with aluminum foil. Place the ribs on the foil, spaced at least 2 inches apart. Broil for 15 minutes, flipping the ribs halfway through.

Using tongs, transfer the ribs to the tomato sauce; discard the fat and juices. Simmer the ribs in the sauce for 1 to 1½ hours, stirring occasionally, until the sauce is thick and the meat is tender and falling apart.

Cook the spaghetti according to the package directions. Drain the spaghetti and place it in a large serving bowl.

Remove the pan from the heat. Remove the ribs to a cutting board and shred the meat with two forks. Discard the bones and return the meat to the pot. Ladle generously over the spaghetti, reserving some to serve on the side.

To make this in a slow cooker:

Eliminate the oil and reduce the beef broth to ¾ cup. Add the onions, crushed tomatoes, beef broth, tomato paste, garlic, parsley, Italian seasoning, oregano, basil, salt, and pepper to the slow cooker. Broil the spareribs as directed above and add them to the slow cooker. Cook for 8 hours on low or 4 hours on high. Uncover the slow cooker and remove the ribs. Proceed with the recipe as above.

1 tablespoon vegetable oil

2 cups chopped onion

1 (28-ounce) can crushed tomatoes in puree

1¾ cups beef broth

1 (6-ounce) can tomato paste

1 tablespoon minced garlic

½ cup loosely packed fresh parsley leaves, chopped

1 tablespoon Italian seasoning

2¼ teaspoons dried oregano

2¼ teaspoons dried basil

2 teaspoons salt

¼ teaspoon pepper

1½ to 2 pounds country-style ribs

12 ounces spaghetti

DEBBIE'S CHICKEN
AND BLACK BEAN ENCHILADAS

Serves 4 to 6

If you try any of the recipes in this book—and I certainly hope you will cook up several!—make sure this one is on your list. It's an often-requested dinner when the family is coming to visit.

This recipe came to me from Joy Fowler, an elementary school teacher who hails from the great state of Texas. Joy was the inspiration for my books The First Man You Meet *and* The Man You'll Marry. *When my daughter Adele was planning her wedding, Joy mailed me a mother-of-the-bride survival package that included a two-pound package of M&M's. I needed it! She also told me these were the best chicken enchiladas, and she's right (though I've taken a few liberties with it over the years).*

3 slices bacon, cut into ½-inch pieces

½ cup diced onion

2 jalapeño chiles, seeded and chopped

1½ teaspoons chopped garlic

12 ounces boneless, skinless chicken breast, sliced into ½-inch strips

¾ teaspoon salt

½ teaspoon black pepper

½ teaspoon chili powder

1 (16-ounce) can black beans, undrained

1 teaspoon ground cumin

1½ cups picante salsa

8 (8-inch) flour tortillas

2½ cups shredded Monterey Jack cheese

(cont'd on next page)

Preheat the oven to 350°F. Grease a 9 x 13-inch baking pan. Line a plate with paper towels.

Cook the bacon in a 12-inch skillet over medium-high heat until crisp, 8 to 10 minutes. Remove the bacon to the prepared plate to drain, leaving the bacon fat in the pan.

Add the onion and cook for 4 to 5 more minutes, until it is soft. Add the garlic and jalapeño and cook for 2 to 3 minutes, until the pepper is soft.

Season the chicken with ½ teaspoon of the salt, the black pepper, and chili powder. Add the chicken to the pan and cook, stirring occasionally, until no longer pink, 6 to 8 minutes.

Stir in the black beans and their liquid, the cumin, the remaining ¼ teaspoon salt, and ½ cup of the salsa. Bring to a simmer and cook, stirring occasionally, until thickened, 7 to 9 minutes. Stir in the cooked bacon.

Spoon ⅓ cup of the chicken and bean mixture down the center of a tortilla. Sprinkle with 2 tablespoons of the cheese. Roll up tightly and place seam-side down in the prepared pan. Repeat with the remaining tortillas. Spread the remaining 1 cup salsa on top of the enchiladas, then top with the remaining cheese.

Bake for 15 to 20 minutes, until the cheese is melted and bubbly. Remove from the oven and serve with the lettuce, tomato, sour cream, and avocado.

Shredded lettuce, for serving

Chopped tomato, for serving

Sour cream, for serving

Sliced avocado, for serving

GREEK CHICKEN PITAS
WITH TZATZIKI SAUCE

Serves 4

Wayne and I enjoy a number of Greek dishes. For this dish, lemony herbed chicken, crunchy veggies, and salty feta are wrapped in a warm, soft pita for a hearty lunch or the perfect warm-weather dinner.

Chicken:
⅓ cup lemon juice
⅓ cup minced fresh mint leaves
2 teaspoons minced garlic
3 tablespoons extra virgin olive oil
1½ teaspoons ground coriander
1½ teaspoons ground cumin
1 teaspoon salt
½ teaspoon pepper
3 boneless, skinless chicken breasts, sliced into ½-inch strips

Marinate the chicken:

In a large bowl, stir together the lemon juice, mint, garlic, olive oil, coriander, cumin, salt, and pepper. Add the chicken and stir to coat with the marinade. Cover and refrigerate for at least 30 minutes or up to 8 hours.

Make the tzatziki sauce:

Set a fine-mesh sieve over a medium bowl. Finely grate the cucumber over the sieve using the small holes of the grater. Push down on the cucumber to extract as much of the juice as possible. Discard the liquid and scoop the grated cucumber into the now-empty bowl. Add the yogurt, garlic, olive oil, vinegar, dill, and salt. Stir well. Cover and refrigerate until ready to serve.

Assemble the pitas:

Preheat the oven to 275°F.

Wrap the pitas in aluminum foil and put them in the oven.

Heat a cast-iron skillet over medium-high heat. Working in two batches, add the chicken and cook for 3 to 4 minutes, flipping halfway through, until the chicken is browned and cooked through.

Remove the pitas from the oven. Spread some tzatziki sauce on each pita, add the chicken, and top with the cheese, tomatoes, and cucumber. Garnish with a swirl of olive oil. Serve with the remaining tzatziki on the side.

Tzatziki sauce:
½ cucumber, peeled
1 cup plain Greek yogurt
¾ teaspoon minced garlic
2 tablespoons extra virgin olive oil
1 tablespoon white vinegar
1 tablespoon minced fresh dill
½ teaspoon salt

4 pita breads
4 ounces feta cheese, crumbled
2 cups halved grape tomatoes
2 cups peeled and diced cucumber
Extra virgin olive oil, for drizzling

You can make the chicken up to a day in advance and assemble the sandwiches when you're ready to eat.

SNOW ON THE MOUNTAIN

Serves 8 to 12

This dish is a New Year's Day tradition with our family. The makings are assembled buffet-style, and each person assembles their own plate. It doesn't seem like the ingredients would go together, but the blend of flavors is absolutely scrumptious.

Chicken:
1 (4- to 5-pound) whole chicken, giblets removed
½ teaspoon salt
¼ teaspoon pepper
1 cup water

Gravy:
3 tablespoons butter
⅓ cup flour
1 cup milk
½ teaspoon salt
⅛ teaspoon pepper

6 to 8 cups cooked rice
4 tomatoes, sliced
2 cups chopped red onion
6 cups crispy chow mein noodles
1 cup chopped celery
1 (7-ounce) can sliced green or black olives, drained
2 cups shredded Cheddar cheese
1 (20-ounce) can crushed pineapple in juice, undrained
1 cup sliced almonds
1½ cups sweetened shredded coconut

Make the chicken:

Pat the chicken dry with paper towels. Season the outside with the salt and pepper. Place in a 6-quart slow cooker and add the water. Cover and cook on high for 4 to 6 hours or low for 6 to 8 hours, until an instant-read thermometer reads 165°F when inserted into the inner thigh.

Remove the chicken to a large cutting board and let cool for 15 minutes. Set aside 2½ cups of the broth from the slow cooker. Shred or dice the meat and place it in a serving bowl. Discard the skin and bones.

Make the gravy:

In a large skillet, melt the butter over medium-high heat. Whisk in the flour and cook for 2 to 3 minutes. Slowly whisk in the reserved broth and the milk. Bring the mixture to a boil, then reduce the heat to medium-low and simmer for 4 to 5 minutes, until thickened. Add the salt and pepper.

Pour over the chicken and gently toss to completely coat it.

To serve:

Place the rice, chicken in gravy, tomatoes, onion, chow mein noodles, celery, olives, cheese, pineapple, almonds, and coconut in serving bowls. Line up the bowls in the order listed.

Each person builds their own "mountain" by layering the ingredients in the proportion that pleases them, beginning with the rice and ending with the coconut.

CARAMELIZED ONION STEAK SLIDERS

Serves 6 to 8

Combine caramelized onions and sliced sirloin to make a steakhouse dinner on a bun. You get steak for dinner and your wallet doesn't take a big hit. Our grandson Carter will eat us out of house and home after a recent growth spurt—these fill him up and keep him coming back for more!

Make the caramelized onions:

In a medium saucepan, melt the butter over medium-low heat. Add the onions and salt and cook for about 30 minutes, stirring occasionally, until the onions are caramelized and medium brown in color.

Preheat the oven to 350°F.

Make the sauce:

In a small bowl, stir together the melted butter, Worcestershire sauce, salt, sugar, garlic powder, and onion powder.

Make the steak:

Season the steak all over with the salt and pepper. Working in batches, cook the slices in a large skillet over high heat for 1 minute on each side. Remove the slices to a platter as they're done.

In a 9 x 13-inch pan, lay the 15 slider bottoms tightly together. Top with the caramelized onions, steak slices, and then the cheese. Top with slider tops.

Brush the sauce over the slider tops and sprinkle with the sesame seeds.

Bake, uncovered, for 15 minutes, or until the cheese is melted. Serve hot.

The sliders can be made and assembled a day ahead of time and stored, covered, in the refrigerator. Make the sauce while the oven is preheating. Brush the mixture on top and sprinkle with sesame seeds just before you put the sliders into the oven. Add 5 minutes to the cooking time.

Place the steak in the freezer for 15 to 20 minutes before slicing. This will make it easier to get thin, even slices.

Caramelized onions:
4 tablespoons (½ stick) butter
2 large onions, thinly sliced
½ teaspoon salt

Sauce:
4 tablespoons (½ stick) butter, melted
1 teaspoon Worcestershire sauce
½ teaspoon salt
¼ teaspoon sugar
¼ teaspoon garlic powder
¼ teaspoon onion powder

Steak:
2 pounds sirloin steak, very thinly sliced
1 teaspoon salt
½ teaspoon pepper

15 slider buns
1 (7-ounce) package (about 3 cups) shredded Swiss or Gruyère cheese
1 tablespoon sesame seeds

TURKEY LETTUCE WRAPS

Serves 4 to 6

You won't believe how fast this comes together and how delicious it is. Who said you had to wait until Thanksgiving to enjoy turkey?

In a large skillet, heat the olive oil over medium-high heat. Add the onion and cook until soft and translucent, about 5 minutes.

Add the turkey and cook, breaking it up with a spoon, until no longer pink, 8 to 10 minutes. Add the mushrooms and bell pepper and cook until soft, 3 to 4 minutes.

Add the garlic and cook for 1 minute, or until fragrant. Add the water chestnuts, hoisin sauce, soy sauce, rice vinegar, ginger, sesame oil, and sriracha and cook for 2 to 3 more minutes.

To serve, divide the turkey mixture evenly among the lettuce leaves. Top with the peanuts and green onions. Drizzle with more sriracha, if desired. Serve warm or at room temperature.

1 tablespoon olive oil

½ cup diced yellow onion

1 pound ground turkey

1 cup chopped mushrooms

⅓ cup diced red bell pepper

2 teaspoons minced garlic

1 (8-ounce) can water chestnuts, drained and chopped

¼ cup hoisin sauce

2 tablespoons soy sauce

2 tablespoons rice vinegar

2 teaspoons grated fresh ginger

1 teaspoon toasted sesame oil

½ teaspoon sriracha, plus more for serving

8 butter lettuce leaves, washed and dried

½ cup chopped roasted unsalted peanuts, for serving

¼ cup sliced green onions or scallions, for garnish

GUINNESS POT PIE

Serves 8 to 10

Pot pie with beer. Do I need say anything more? Every hero in every book I've ever written would want to sample this dish.

2 pounds beef chuck roast, cut into 1-inch cubes

½ teaspoon salt, plus more to taste

¾ teaspoon pepper, plus more to taste

2 tablespoons vegetable oil

1 large onion, diced (about 2½ cups)

3 stalks celery, diced (about 1½ cups)

8 ounces mushrooms, cleaned, stems trimmed, and quartered (about 2¾ cups)

1 tablespoon minced garlic

2 tablespoons tomato paste

¼ cup flour

1 teaspoon dried thyme

½ teaspoon dried rosemary

2 cups Guinness

1 cup beef broth

1 (17.3-ounce) box frozen puff pastry

3 cups diced russet potatoes

1 (12-ounce) package frozen peas and carrots (2½ cups)

1 egg

1 tablespoon water

Season the beef with the salt and pepper. Heat 1 tablespoon of the oil in a large saucepan over medium-high heat. Working in two batches, brown the beef on all sides, 2 to 3 minutes per side, for a total of 8 to 10 minutes. Remove the beef with a slotted spoon to a bowl. Leave the juices and browned bits in the pot.

Heat the remaining 1 tablespoon oil in the same pan. Add the onion, celery, and mushrooms and cook until the onion is translucent, 5 to 7 minutes. Add the garlic and cook until fragrant, about 1 minute. Stir in the tomato paste, flour, thyme, and rosemary and cook, stirring constantly, for 2 minutes. Stir in the Guinness and beef broth, scraping up any browned bits from the bottom of the pot. Add the beef and any juices from the bowl, then bring to a boil. Reduce the heat to low, cover, and simmer for 1 hour, stirring occasionally.

Remove the puff pastry from the freezer. Preheat the oven to 425°F.

Add the potatoes to the pot and bring back to a boil over medium-high heat. Reduce the heat to low and simmer, uncovered, until fork tender, about 30 minutes. Stir in the peas and carrots. Season with salt and pepper.

Ladle the pot pie filling into eight 10-ounce oven-safe ramekins or two 1½- to 2-quart oven-safe shallow baking dishes. They will not be completely full. If you're using ramekins, place them on a rimmed baking sheet for easy transport to and from the oven.

Cut the puff pastry into circles a little bigger than each dish. Drape the pastry on top of each dish and press lightly so it adheres to the edges. In a small bowl, whisk the egg with the water and brush the egg wash over the tops of the pastry.

Bake for 18 to 20 minutes, until the puff pastry is golden brown and puffed. Remove from the oven and serve immediately.

You can prepare the filling the day before and assemble and bake the pies right before serving. Remove the puff pastry from the freezer 30 minutes before assembling.

Freeze the large pie without the puff pastry topping for up to 1 month. Defrost in the refrigerator, top with the puff pastry, and bake as directed in the recipe.

Individual pot pies can be frozen completely assembled for up to 1 month. They do not have to be defrosted. Preheat the oven to 425°F and bake for 30 to 40 minutes, until the filling is hot and the crust is golden.

Don't use precut stew meat. Not only is cutting up a chuck roast less expensive, the quality of the meat will be better. And if you don't drink alcohol, just substitute another 2 cups of beef stock for the Guinness.

BACON-WRAPPED MEATLOAF

Serves 6 to 8

Kick your meatloaf up a notch by wrapping it in bacon! But then, who can refuse anything with bacon?

Preheat the oven to 350°F. Line a rimmed baking sheet with aluminum foil or parchment paper.

Heat the olive oil in a medium skillet over medium-high heat. Add the onion and cook until soft and translucent, about 5 minutes. Remove the pan from the heat and let cool.

In a large bowl, mix together the eggs, parsley, salt, pepper, garlic, saltines, and milk until well combined. Add the beef, pork, and onion and mix with your hands just until combined. Transfer the mixture to the prepared baking sheet and form it into a rectangle roughly measuring 9 inches long and 5 inches wide.

In a small bowl, mix together the ketchup, brown sugar, vinegar, and mustard. Pour half of the glaze into a small bowl and set aside to serve with the meatloaf. Set aside 1 tablespoon of the remaining glaze. Brush the rest of the glaze all over the meatloaf.

Lay the strips of bacon crosswise on top of the meatloaf, overlapping each piece slightly until you have covered the meatloaf completely. Tuck the ends of the strips under the meatloaf. Bake for 60 to 70 minutes, until an instant-read thermometer inserted in the center of the meatloaf reads 155°F. Remove the meatloaf from the oven.

Position the rack as close to the broiler as possible. Preheat the broiler.

Brush the bacon with the reserved 1 tablespoon glaze, then broil for 2 to 4 minutes, until the glaze is bubbling and the bacon is crisp. Remove the meatloaf from the oven and let it cool for 5 minutes. Slice and serve with the remaining glaze.

1 tablespoon olive oil

1 cup coarsely chopped onion

2 eggs

⅓ cup chopped fresh parsley

1 teaspoon salt

½ teaspoon pepper

2 teaspoons minced garlic

⅔ cup crushed saltines

⅓ cup milk

1¼ pounds ground beef

12 ounces ground pork

½ cup ketchup

5 tablespoons brown sugar

2 tablespoons apple cider vinegar

½ teaspoon dry mustard

12 slices bacon

LAYERED BEEF ENCHILADA CASSEROLE

Serves 8 to 10

Mexican food has long been a family favorite. This casserole gives you all the flavor of enchiladas without the need to roll up each tortilla. Make sure to bake this uncovered, so the tortillas on top get nice and crispy.

1 tablespoon vegetable oil

2½ cups diced onion

1 pound ground beef

1½ teaspoons minced garlic

1 packet taco seasoning

1 (15.25-ounce) can corn, drained

1 (4.5-ounce) can diced green chiles, drained

2 (2.25-ounce) cans sliced black olives, drained

1 (10-ounce) can red enchilada sauce

14 corn tortillas

1 (16-ounce) package shredded Mexican cheese blend

Sour cream, for garnish

Chopped fresh cilantro, for garnish

Heat the vegetable oil in a large skillet over medium-high heat. Add the onion and cook until translucent and soft, 4 to 5 minutes. Add the ground beef and cook, stirring to break it up, until crumbly and no longer pink, 6 to 8 minutes.

Add the garlic and taco seasoning, stir to combine, and cook for 2 minutes. Remove the pan from the heat and stir in the corn, green chiles, and one can of olives. Stir in ¾ cup of the enchilada sauce and reserve the rest.

Preheat the oven to 375°F.

Spread ¼ cup of the reserved enchilada sauce over a 9 x 13-inch baking dish. Top with 4 tortillas. Spread half of the beef mixture on top. Sprinkle on 1½ cups of the cheese. Repeat the layers with 4 more tortillas, the remaining beef mixture, and 1½ cups of the cheese. Top with the remaining 6 tortillas, the remaining ½ cup enchilada sauce, and the rest of the cheese. Sprinkle the remaining can of sliced olives evenly over the top.

Bake, uncovered, for 30 minutes, or until bubbling and the cheese is melted.

Remove the casserole from the oven and let cool on a wire rack for 5 minutes. Cut into squares and serve with the sour cream and cilantro.

MOZZARELLA-STUFFED MEATBALLS

Makes 24

I find meatballs to be so versatile. These can be served in a roll, warmed in pasta sauce, or as is, accompanied by a simple green vegetable like broccoli. However you choose to use them, they are sure to satisfy.

Line a rimmed baking sheet with aluminum foil or parchment paper.

In a large bowl, mix together the breadcrumbs, cheese, eggs, basil, garlic, salt, and pepper. Add the sausage and mix well. Add the ground beef and gently mix just until combined. Divide the mixture into 24 equal portions of about 2 tablespoons each and place on the prepared baking sheet.

Cut each stick of string cheese into 8 even pieces. Push a piece in the center of a portion of meat and pinch it closed. Roll into a ball. Repeat with the remaining string cheese and portions of meat. Cover with plastic wrap and refrigerate the meatballs on the baking sheet for at least 30 minutes or up to 12 hours.

Preheat the oven to 350°F.

In a large nonstick skillet, brown the meatballs over medium-high heat on all sides, about 10 minutes. Don't overcrowd the pan, otherwise the meatballs won't brown or steam properly. You may need to do this in two or three batches. When each batch is done, return them to the baking sheet. When all the meatballs are browned, bake them for 18 to 20 minutes, until the meatballs are cooked through.

¾ cup panko breadcrumbs

½ cup shredded Parmesan cheese

2 eggs

1½ teaspoons dried basil

1½ teaspoons minced garlic

1 teaspoon salt

½ teaspoon pepper

8 ounces ground sweet Italian sausage

1 pound 85% lean ground beef

3 sticks string cheese

2 tablespoons vegetable oil

These meatballs freeze beautifully, and you can reheat them in the oven or in sauce directly from the freezer.

STANDING RIB ROAST

Serves 6 to 8

This recipe is simple but makes a special meal even more special. Wayne isn't overly fond of turkey, so every Thanksgiving I cook two big dinners. Not every family member can join us on Thanksgiving, so the night before I serve a rib roast for Wayne and whoever else can attend. We call it our Day Before Thanksgiving Feast.

2 teaspoons salt
1 teaspoon pepper
1 teaspoon garlic powder
1 (5- to 6-pound) standing beef rib roast

Preheat the oven to 350°F.

In a small bowl, mix the salt, pepper, and garlic powder together.

Place the roast on a roasting rack set in a shallow pan, rib-side down. Rub the spice mixture all over the roast.

Roast for 2 to 2½ hours, until an instant-read thermometer inserted into the thickest part of the roast reads 145°F. Do not let the thermometer touch the bone.

Remove the roast from the oven, cover loosely with aluminum foil, and let rest for at least 15 minutes before carving.

EASY SLOW COOKER PULLED PORK

Serves 12

I use my slow cooker so often I leave it sitting on the kitchen counter. One of our most loved recipes is this one for pulled pork. It's incredibly versatile: for starters, use the pork in sandwiches or tacos or on top of nachos.

Place the onions and garlic in the bottom of a 6-quart slow cooker. Place the pork roast on top.

In a small bowl, mix together the chili powder, brown sugar, salt, cinnamon, cumin, and pepper. Rub the spice mixture all over the pork. Cover and cook on high for 6 to 7 hours or on low for 9 to 10 hours. Transfer the roast to a cutting board and shred with two forks.

Place the pork in a serving bowl or rimmed platter. Add the cooking liquid to the pork until it's as juicy as you like.

Serving Suggestions

BBQ Pulled Pork Sandwiches: Pile the pulled pork on soft buns and top with your favorite barbecue sauce and coleslaw.

Pulled Pork Tacos: Top warmed corn tortillas with pulled pork, salsa, sliced or diced avocado, and queso fresco.

Pulled Pork Nachos: Place a single layer of tortilla chips on an aluminum foil–lined rimmed baking sheet. Layer pulled pork, Cheddar cheese, and diced red onion on top. Broil on high for 3 to 4 minutes, until the cheese is melted. Remove from the oven and sprinkle with chopped tomatoes and sliced jalapeños.

2 red or yellow onions, sliced

4 garlic cloves, peeled and smashed

1 (4- to 5-pound) bone-in pork shoulder roast

4 teaspoons chili powder

1 tablespoon brown sugar

1 tablespoon salt

½ teaspoon ground cinnamon

½ teaspoon ground cumin

½ teaspoon pepper

You can keep the pulled pork in the refrigerator, covered, for up to 5 days. Freeze the pork in its juices in small portions for up to 4 months for dinner in a jiffy. Reheat in the microwave or on the stovetop.

HERB ROASTED LAMB CHOPS
WITH DIJON-ROSEMARY SAUCE

Serves 4

It's only been in the last few years that I started eating lamb. I had no idea how flavorful it is! If you've never tasted lamb, give this a try. Serve it with steamed peas and boiled new potatoes for a special dinner with friends.

Make the lamb chops:

Preheat the oven to 400°F. Sprinkle both sides of the lamb chops evenly with the oregano, rosemary, salt, and pepper.

Heat the oil in a large ovenproof skillet over high heat. Add the lamb and brown for 3 minutes on each side. Transfer the skillet to the oven or transfer the lamb to a rimmed baking sheet and roast for 10 minutes, or until an instant-read thermometer inserted in the middle of a chop reaches 135°F. Transfer the lamb to a platter, cover loosely with aluminum foil, and let rest for 10 minutes.

Make the sauce:

In a small saucepan, whisk together the half-and-half, mustard, and rosemary. Heat over medium heat until hot, but do not let it boil. Season with salt and pepper.

Place the lamb chops on a serving platter and spoon some of the sauce over the chops. Serve the remaining sauce on the side.

Lamb chops:
4 (1-inch-thick) lamb loin chops
2 teaspoons dried oregano
2 teaspoons dried rosemary, lightly crushed
½ teaspoon salt
¼ teaspoon pepper
2 tablespoons vegetable oil

Dijon-rosemary sauce:
1 cup half-and-half
3 tablespoons Dijon mustard
½ teaspoon dried rosemary
Salt and pepper

SPICY PORK CHOPS

Serves 4

Don't let the title of this recipe scare you; these chops are well seasoned but not overly spicy. If you like more heat, you can add a little more chili powder; if you prefer it milder, use less.

Serve this with rice or mashed potatoes to sop up the delicious pan juices.

2 tablespoons chili powder
1 tablespoon paprika
1½ teaspoons salt
½ teaspoon garlic powder
½ teaspoon onion powder
4 (1½-inch-thick) boneless pork chops
1 tablespoon vegetable oil

Preheat the oven to 400°F.

In a shallow pan, mix together the chili powder, paprika, salt, garlic powder, and onion powder. Press each pork chop into the spice mixture, generously coating them on all sides.

In a 12-inch oven-safe skillet, heat the oil over medium-high heat until shimmering. Fry the pork chops for 4 to 5 minutes on the first side and 3 to 4 minutes on the second side, until each side is well browned. Transfer the skillet, uncovered, to the oven and roast for 10 to 12 minutes, until an instant-read thermometer reads 145°F when inserted in the center of a chop.

Remove the skillet from the oven, cover the pan with a tight-fitting lid or aluminum foil, and let the chops rest for 5 minutes. Place the chops on a platter, pour the pan juices over all and serve immediately.

HONEY-CHIPOTLE OVEN-ROASTED RIBS

Serves 6

Our son-in-law, Greg Banks, is the rib man in our family. His barbecued ribs are the best. When the weather is crummy and the outdoor barbecue/smoker isn't accessible, he easily transitions to the oven with this recipe. No doubt Sam Carney, from If Not for You, *ordered up ribs just like these with his friends from the garage after a long workweek.*

Preheat the oven to 400°F. Cover a rimmed baking sheet with a long piece of aluminum foil that hangs over the ends at least 2 inches. Place two pieces of foil crosswise to overhang the sides at least 6 inches on both sides.

In a small bowl, combine the chipotles, ¼ cup of the honey, the mustard, pepper, and salt.

Lay the ribs meaty-side up in the middle of the foil and spread the chipotle mixture all over the top. Wrap the ribs tightly in the foil and bake for 2 to 2½ hours, until fork tender.

Remove the ribs from the oven and preheat the broiler. Open the foil and roll it back to expose the top of the ribs.

Spread the remaining ⅓ cup honey all over the top of the ribs. Broil for 3 to 5 minutes, until the honey is bubbling and the ribs are lightly charred. Cut between the bones into serving-size portions or individual ribs and serve immediately.

¼ cup minced canned chipotle chiles in adobo
¼ cup plus ⅓ cup honey
¼ cup powdered mustard
1½ teaspoons pepper
3 tablespoons salt
5 pounds pork spareribs

Any cut of ribs will work here. You can cook the ribs a day in advance and heat them under the broiler right before serving.

ASPARAGUS TOMATO QUICHE

Serves 8

This colorful vegetable pie is equally at home for lunch, at brunch, or on the dinner table. I'm here to tell you that real men and boys do eat quiche. Just ask the men in my family.

Preheat the oven to 450°F. Line a rimmed baking sheet with aluminum foil or parchment paper.

Place the asparagus on the foil and toss with the olive oil. Spread the pieces out evenly and sprinkle with 1 teaspoon of the salt and ½ teaspoon of the pepper. Roast for 7 to 9 minutes, until fork tender. Remove the sheet from the oven and let cool for about 5 minutes.

Reduce the oven temperature to 375°F.

Line a 9-inch pie plate with the piecrust. Spread the roasted asparagus evenly over the bottom, then layer the tomatoes over the asparagus. Sprinkle the cheese over all.

In a medium bowl, whisk the eggs lightly to break up the yolks. Whisk in the milk, cream, the remaining 1 teaspoon salt, and the remaining ½ teaspoon pepper. Pour the mixture over the vegetables and cheese and sprinkle the green onions evenly on top.

Place the pie pan on a rimmed baking sheet in case the quiche overflows.

Bake for 40 to 50 minutes, until a knife inserted 1 inch from the edge comes out clean. Transfer to a wire rack to cool. Serve warm or at room temperature.

1 bunch asparagus (about 1 pound), ends trimmed and cut into 1-inch pieces

1 tablespoon olive oil

2 teaspoons salt

1 teaspoon pepper

1 (9-inch) refrigerated piecrust

1 cup halved red or yellow grape tomatoes

1½ cups shredded Swiss cheese

4 eggs

1 cup milk

⅔ cup cream

¼ cup sliced green onions or scallions

SALAMI AND SPINACH STROMBOLI

Serves 4

Here's a quick weeknight dinner idea: just thaw the spinach in the microwave and use your favorite store-bought marinara sauce and pre-shredded cheese.

A 9-ounce package of frozen spinach is about 1 cup thawed. So why not double the recipe? If you have teenage boys or grandsons in the house, the stromboli will disappear in one sitting.

1 (13.8-ounce) tube pizza dough

Flour, for dusting

½ cup marinara sauce, plus more for serving

1½ teaspoons minced garlic

⅛ teaspoon crushed red pepper flakes

¼ teaspoon coarse salt

⅛ teaspoon black pepper

½ cup frozen chopped spinach, thawed and drained

4 ounces salami, sliced into strips

1½ cups shredded mozzarella cheese

These will keep in the refrigerator for a couple of days. Or freeze after baking and reheat in the toaster oven.

Preheat the oven to 350°F. Line a rimmed baking sheet with parchment paper.

Unroll the dough onto a lightly floured work surface. Cut the dough in half lengthwise and crosswise, making four even rectangles.

Press each piece out gently to make 7 x 5-inch rectangles.

Divide the marinara sauce evenly over the pieces of dough, spreading it so it covers the dough with ½ inch of space left uncovered on both short ends of each piece of dough. Sprinkle with the garlic, red pepper flakes, salt, and black pepper. Layer the spinach, salami, and cheese over the top of the four pieces.

Roll each piece of dough up lengthwise and place on the prepared baking sheet seam-side down. Make 2 or 3 small cuts in the top of each stromboli.

Bake for 25 to 30 minutes, until the stromboli are golden brown. Serve immediately, with extra marinara sauce.

DEEP-DISH PIZZA

Serves 6

I'm convinced I have Italian blood in me somewhere. Pasta and pizza call my name! Pizza comes up a lot in my books, Starry Night *being a perfect example. Because of course Carrie had to take Finn to eat deep-dish pizza when he visited her in Chicago.*

I once went on a diet (one of about a thousand), in which I didn't eat anything that started with a "p," because all my weakness food were "p" words—pizza, popcorn, pasta, peanut butter. . . .

If you want a meatless version, leave off the pepperoni and add a layer of your favorite veggie: thawed, drained frozen spinach, sliced mushrooms, peppers, tomatoes, olives, artichoke hearts, and fresh basil leaves are all delicious.

1½ cups warm (about 110°F) water

1 (¼-ounce) packet active dry yeast

1 teaspoon sugar

½ cup semolina flour

1 teaspoon salt

½ cup olive oil, plus 3 teaspoons for oiling the bowl and pan

3½ cups all-purpose flour, plus additional for dusting

1½ cups shredded mozzarella cheese

1 (3.5-ounce) package pepperoni slices

1½ cups pizza sauce

Make the dough:

In a large bowl, combine the water, yeast, and sugar. Stir to combine. Let sit until foamy, about 5 minutes.

Add the semolina flour, salt, ½ cup of the olive oil, and 2 cups of the all-purpose flour. Mix with a wooden spoon until smooth. Continue to stir in the rest of the flour, ½ cup at a time, until it is all incorporated.

Turn the dough out onto a lightly floured surface and knead it with your hands until smooth, 3 to 4 minutes.

Oil a large bowl with 2 teaspoons of the remaining olive oil. Place the dough in the bowl and turn it a few times so the dough is coated with oil on all sides. Cover the bowl with a dish towel and set in a warm place until almost doubled in size, about 1½ hours.

Assemble and bake the pizza:

Preheat the oven to 450°F.

Dip a paper towel in the remaining 1 teaspoon olive oil

and use it to coat the inside of a 4-quart Dutch oven or 12-inch cast-iron skillet. Place the dough inside the pan and stretch it to fit the bottom of the pan by pushing gently with your fingers. Let the dough rest for 5 minutes, then stretch it again, pushing the dough at least 2 inches up the sides of the pan.

Sprinkle the cheese over the dough. Layer on the pepperoni, then pour the sauce over the top. Bake for about 30 minutes, until the crust is golden brown and the cheese is bubbling. Remove the pan from the oven and let cool for 5 minutes. Cut into 6 slices and serve immediately.

You can use the Tomato Dipping Sauce (page 37) or your favorite commercial or homemade pizza sauce.

The semolina flour gives the dough a slight crunch. You can find semolina flour in the baking or natural foods section of your supermarket. It can also be found in the bulk bin section.

PEANUT BUTTER NOODLES
WITH THAI FLAVORS AND CRISPY TOFU

Serves 4 to 6

I'm a peanut butter nut and am willing to try any recipe that calls for it as an ingredient. Our granddaughters, Bailey and Maddy, are vegetarians and have introduced me to the delights of tofu. Who knew? It's actually quite good, especially if there's peanut butter involved.

Line a rimmed baking sheet with a double layer of paper towels. Cut the tofu lengthwise into ½-inch slices, then cut crosswise into 1-inch pieces. Place on the baking sheet and press with more paper towels to dry the tofu until no moisture remains.

In a medium bowl, whisk the peanut butter with the water until smooth. Whisk in the soy sauce, honey, sesame oil, lime juice, ginger, and garlic.

Bring a large pot of water to a boil. Add the linguine and cook according to the package directions. Drain and place in a large serving bowl.

While the pasta is cooking, toss the tofu in the cornstarch and shake off the excess.

Heat the oil in a 12-inch skillet over medium-high heat until hot and shimmering. Fry the tofu until golden brown and very crispy, 4 to 5 minutes per side. Remove to a paper towel–lined plate. Discard the oil.

In the same skillet, heat the sauce with the carrots, bell pepper, and noodles over medium heat until heated through. Add the tofu and toss everything together. Serve hot, garnished with the green onions and peanuts.

1 (1-pound) block extra-firm tofu

¾ cup creamy peanut butter

¼ cup warm water

¼ cup soy sauce

2 tablespoons honey

1 tablespoon toasted sesame oil

2 tablespoons lime juice

4 teaspoons minced fresh ginger

1 tablespoon minced garlic

12 ounces linguini noodles

½ cup cornstarch

¼ cup canola oil

1 cup shredded carrots

½ red bell pepper, seeded and cut into matchsticks

¼ cup thinly sliced green onions or scallions

¼ cup unsalted roasted peanuts, chopped

You can substitute an equal amount of almond butter for the peanut butter. Add an additional 2 to 3 tablespoons honey and garnish with chopped toasted almonds.

SPINACH-ARTICHOKE LASAGNA

Serves 8 to 10

If you love spinach-artichoke dip, you'll love this lasagna. It's versatile! Leave the bacon out, and it's a vegetarian dish, or swap in mozzarella for the Monterey Jack or add chicken (see the variation below).

Try it with the Kale Caesar Salad (page 64).

10 lasagna noodles

1 (16-ounce) container cottage cheese

3 eggs

1 (9-ounce) box frozen chopped spinach, thawed and squeezed dry

1 (9-ounce) box frozen artichoke hearts, thawed and chopped

1 teaspoon salt

¼ teaspoon pepper

½ teaspoon garlic powder

10 slices bacon, cut into 1-inch slices

2 pounds Monterey Jack cheese, shredded

1 cup shredded Parmesan cheese

Cook the lasagna noodles according to the package directions. Drain.

Preheat the oven to 350°F.

In a medium bowl, whisk together the cottage cheese and eggs.

In a large bowl, stir together the spinach, artichoke hearts, salt, pepper, and garlic powder.

In a large skillet, cook the bacon over medium heat until soft, about 5 minutes. Do not let it crisp. Remove to a paper towel–lined plate to drain.

Layer half of the noodles over a 9 x 13-inch baking pan. Spread half of the cottage cheese mixture over them. Make a layer of half of the vegetable mixture, then half of the Monterey Jack cheese, then half of the Parmesan cheese. Repeat the layers and spread the bacon evenly over all.

Bake for 30 to 35 minutes, until the cheese is bubbling and the bacon is crisp. Remove from the oven and let cool for 10 minutes before serving.

Variation:

Chicken Spinach-Artichoke Lasagna: Add 4 cups chopped cooked chicken: spread 2 cups over each layer of the vegetable mixture and proceed with the other layers.

SIDES

As you might expect, my entire family is a bunch of foodies. Guess you could say the acorns fall close to the tree, and we love to cook as much as we love to eat. Because we have been blessed with a weekend house on the water, the family gathers together nearly every weekend. Our waterfront has an abundance of seafood: oysters, clams, shrimp, and crab. I never have to worry about snacks or appetizers at our weekend home because the kids and grandkids invariably arrive with a plethora of goodies. It's been that way from the first family potluck. I toss ribs on the grill and everything else is supplied by the kids: side dishes galore. Recipes to share. Rave reviews as we pass them around. Ted and family bring my dad's recipe for potato salad; Laurie supplies her special rice dish—she dare not show up without it! In fact, several of the recipes shared in this collection come from my children.

Potlucks are our favorite family times, and it's no different over the holidays, either. Everyone contributes, each family eagerly sharing a special side dish. Sides for us are far more than a mere accompaniment of the meal. The dishes that each family member brings to the gathering are a way of giving a part of themselves to share with the rest of us.

CAMERON'S GARLIC
AND BACON GREEN BEANS

Serves 4 to 6

From the time our oldest grandson, Cameron, was a toddler, green beans have been his all-time favorite vegetable. I make sure to serve them whenever he comes to dinner.

2 pounds green beans, trimmed

⅔ cup water

8 slices bacon, cut into 1-inch pieces

2 teaspoons minced garlic

2 tablespoons butter

2 tablespoons brown sugar

¼ teaspoon salt

In a 12-inch skillet, heat the beans in the water over high heat until boiling. Continue to boil, stirring constantly, until the water has completely evaporated, about 5 minutes.

Reduce the heat to medium-high, push the beans to the outside of the pan, and put the bacon in the middle. Fry for 4 to 5 minutes, until crisp. Add the garlic and stir all the ingredients together. Cook for 1 minute, or until the garlic is fragrant.

Stir in the butter, brown sugar, and salt into the green beans and bacon and cook until the butter melts and the brown sugar dissolves, about 2 minutes. Remove to a serving dish and serve hot.

GRILLED CORN
WITH SWEET AND SPICY BUTTER

Serves 4

This is one of Wayne's all-time favorite recipes. Adding the sweet-spicy butter gives the grilled corn an extra kick. I need to double the recipe for Wayne, who would happily eat the entire bowl and skip whatever else I'm serving.

In a small bowl, mash the butter with a fork. Add the brown sugar, cayenne, salt, and black pepper and mix until well combined.

Prepare a charcoal grill or heat a gas grill to medium-high. Grill the corn for 8 to 10 minutes, turning a few times to cook it evenly on all sides.

Remove the corn from the grill, brush it with the prepared butter, and serve immediately.

6 tablespoons (¾ cup) butter, at room temperature

2 tablespoons brown sugar

¼ teaspoon cayenne pepper

½ teaspoon salt

¼ teaspoon black pepper

4 ears yellow corn, husks removed

You can make the butter ahead of time and keep it covered in the fridge; it will keep for up to 1 month. It will keep frozen for up to 6 months. Bring it to room temperature, covered, before serving. It's nice to have on hand to melt over frozen or canned corn when you can't get fresh in season.

ROASTED SESAME ASPARAGUS

Serves 4 to 6

Yakima is situated in the center of Washington State, an extremely productive agricultural region. When I was growing up, having fresh produce on the table was the norm, and when asparagus was in season, Mom cooked it in a variety of ways. Roasting was—and is—by far my favorite.

1 bunch asparagus (about 1 pound), tough ends trimmed
1 tablespoon olive oil
½ teaspoon salt
1½ teaspoons sesame seeds

Preheat the oven to 450°F.

On a rimmed baking sheet, toss the asparagus with the olive oil. Sprinkle the salt over all. Bake for 10 minutes.

Remove the baking sheet from the oven and sprinkle the asparagus with the sesame seeds. Bake for 5 to 7 more minutes, until the asparagus is fork tender and the sesame seeds are lightly toasted. Serve hot, warm, or at room temperature.

DEBBIE'S ZUCCHINI WITH BACON, ONIONS, AND JALAPEÑO OVER MASHED POTATOES

Serves 4 to 6

This recipe is another family favorite. It's based on my mom's recipe for tomato gravy; I took her recipe and jazzed it up as a way to get my kids to eat zucchini. It worked! But I didn't add the jalapeño until they were older.

In a large skillet, cook the bacon over medium-high heat until crisp, 8 to 10 minutes. Remove the bacon to a paper towel–lined plate and pour the grease into a heatproof bowl.

Return 1 tablespoon of the bacon grease to the skillet and heat over medium-high heat. Add the onion and cook for 3 to 4 minutes, until translucent and soft.

Add the zucchini and cook for 6 to 7 minutes, stirring frequently, until the zucchini starts to get soft. Add the jalapeño and garlic and cook for 1 to 2 minutes, until fragrant.

Add the tomato juice, bring to a simmer, then reduce the heat to medium-low and cook, stirring occasionally, for 5 to 7 minutes, until the juice has thickened and the zucchini is very soft. Add the salt and pepper. Serve over mashed potatoes topped with the bacon.

8 ounces bacon slices, cut into ½-inch strips

1 cup chopped onion

5 cups thinly sliced zucchini

2 tablespoons minced jalapeño chile (about 1 small)

1½ teaspoons minced garlic

1 cup tomato juice

½ teaspoon salt

¼ teaspoon pepper

Your favorite recipe for mashed potatoes

CHEDDAR GARLIC STUFFED POTATOES

Serves 4

Rich and cheesy, these potatoes are worth the extra time and effort. So when I make them it's a real treat. You can stuff them a day ahead and keep them covered in the refrigerator.

They'd be great alongside a simple grilled steak or roasted chicken. Or try them with the Spicy Pork Chops (page 98) or Standing Rib Roast (page 94).

4 large russet potatoes, scrubbed

4 tablespoons (½ stick) butter, at room temperature

1 head garlic

1 tablespoon olive oil

1⅓ cups shredded Cheddar cheese

⅓ cup sour cream

¼ cup minced fresh chives

¾ teaspoon salt

½ teaspoon pepper

Preheat the oven to 400°F. Line a rimmed baking sheet with aluminum foil.

Pierce the potatoes all over with a fork. Rub the potatoes with 1 tablespoon of the butter. Wrap each potato in foil.

Slice off the top third of the head of garlic so that each clove is exposed. Discard the top. Place the head on a piece of foil and drizzle with the olive oil. Close the foil around the garlic.

Place the potatoes and garlic in the oven and bake the potatoes for about 1 hour, until tender. Bake the garlic for 45 to 55 minutes, until the center cloves are soft when pierced with a knife. Remove from the oven and let cool for 10 minutes.

Squeeze the garlic cloves into a large bowl. Add the remaining 3 tablespoons butter, 1 cup of the cheese, the sour cream, 2 tablespoons of the chives, the salt, and pepper. Mash everything together with a fork until completely combined.

Remove the potatoes from the foil. Slice the tops off the potatoes lengthwise and discard. Carefully scoop out the flesh into the bowl with the garlic mixture, leaving a thin shell intact. Mash the potatoes with the other filling ingredients until smooth. Stuff each potato with the mixture.

Place the potatoes on the prepared baking sheet and sprinkle with the remaining ⅓ cup cheese and the remaining 2 tablespoons chives. Bake for 20 to 25 minutes, until heated through.

ADLER POTATO SALAD

Serves 6 to 8

My dad loved potato salad. (Now that I think about it, he loved anything *with potatoes!) Mom dutifully made a huge bowl for him every week. I was married before I learned that not everyone had potato salad for breakfast!*

This recipe has been in our family for years, although I add pickles from time to time. The jalapeño is my cousin Cherie's idea.

Place the potatoes in a large pot and cover with water. Bring to a boil over high heat. Reduce the heat and simmer for 30 to 40 minutes, until the potatoes are fork tender. Drain the potatoes and rinse with cold water until the potatoes are cool enough to handle. Cut them into 1-inch cubes.

In a large serving bowl, combine the onion, jalapeño, mayonnaise, Miracle Whip, mustard, salt, pepper, and seasoning salt until well blended.

Slice 3 of the eggs and set aside. Chop the remaining 4 eggs and add to the mayonnaise mixture. Gently fold in the potatoes.

Fan out the reserved egg slices across the top of the serving bowl and sprinkle all over with paprika and parsley.

3 pounds russet potatoes, peeled

½ cup minced onion

2 tablespoons minced jalapeño chile (about 1 small)

¾ cup mayonnaise

¾ cup Miracle Whip

1 tablespoon yellow mustard

¾ teaspoon salt

¾ teaspoon pepper

½ teaspoon seasoning salt

7 hard-boiled eggs, peeled

Paprika, for garnish

Chopped fresh parsley, for garnish

BAKED POLENTA FRIES

Serves 4 to 6

I only recently discovered polenta and am enjoying experimenting with it. One idea was these fries. Crunchy on the outside and creamy on the inside, they are a nice change from French fries. Try this as a side to the Spicy Pork Chops (page 98).

2 tubes precooked polenta, cut into ½-inch-wide, 3-inch-long spears

2 tablespoons olive oil

¾ cup shredded Parmesan cheese

2 tablespoons chopped fresh rosemary

¾ teaspoon salt

½ teaspoon pepper

Preheat the oven to 450°F. Line two rimmed baking sheets with aluminum foil or parchment paper.

In a large bowl, toss the polenta with the olive oil. Spread it evenly on the prepared baking sheets. Sprinkle with the cheese, rosemary, salt, and pepper.

Bake for 30 to 35 minutes, flipping the spears halfway through, until crispy and golden. Drain them on paper towels and serve immediately.

You can find tubes of precooked polenta in the Italian foods or natural foods section of your supermarket.

LAURIE'S RICE

Makes 8 cups

My daughter-in-law, Laurie, is the widow of my son, Dale, and the mother of my grandson, Jaxon. She remains a big part of our family and has a reputation for bringing the best dishes to our family gatherings. Two of her special recipes are included in this cookbook.

Our family has been known to fight over this rice—that's how good it is! Laurie makes as much as her rice cooker will hold and brings it to all our family dinners. She dare not forget! I've made it several times on my own, but it never seems to taste as good as Laurie's. I believe she adds an extra ingredient: love.

In a large pot, bring the water to a boil over high heat. Stir in the rice and bring back to a simmer. Cover, reduce the heat to low, and cook until all the liquid has evaporated and the rice is tender, 15 to 20 minutes for white rice and 25 to 30 minutes for brown rice. Fluff with a fork.

Stir the sugar and soy sauce into the hot rice until the sugar is melted. Stir in the bacon and green onions until well combined. Serve hot.

6 cups water

3 cups white or brown rice

⅔ cup sugar

¾ cup soy sauce

1 pound bacon, cooked and crumbled

1¾ cups chopped green onions or scallions

BACON MACARONI AND CHEESE

Serves 8

Bacon, cheese, and pasta? Now really—who could resist this combination? Adding sour cream to the cheese sauce gives this dish that extra creaminess.

This would be perfect on a summer barbecue table or accompanying Honey-Chipotle Oven-Roasted Ribs (page 99). You could also serve it with a crisp green salad or with some carrot and celery sticks and call it a meal.

5 slices white sandwich bread, with or without crusts, as you and your family prefer

3 tablespoons cold butter, cubed

1 pound elbow macaroni

1 pound bacon, coarsely chopped

6 tablespoons flour

1½ teaspoons dry mustard

¼ teaspoon cayenne pepper

½ teaspoon paprika

1 teaspoon salt

4 cups milk

1 cup sour cream

2½ cups shredded sharp Cheddar cheese

2 cups shredded Monterey Jack cheese

Make this a day in advance and store covered in foil in the refrigerator. Let the dish come to room temperature. Preheat the oven to 400°F and bake for 35 to 40 minutes. Remove the foil and broil for 3 to 5 minutes.

Preheat the broiler. Grease a 9 x 13-inch baking dish.

Tear the bread into large pieces. In a food processor, pulse the bread and butter until you have coarse crumbs.

Cook the macaroni according to the instructions on the package until tender. Drain.

Dry out the pot and cook the bacon in the same pot over medium-high heat until crisp, 8 to 10 minutes. Using a slotted spoon, remove all of the bacon and drain it on paper towels. Pour the bacon fat into a heatproof bowl, then spoon 5 tablespoons of the fat back into the pot.

Heat the bacon fat over medium-high heat and whisk in the flour, mustard, cayenne, paprika, and salt. Cook for 1 minute, whisking constantly. Slowly whisk in the milk and sour cream until smooth. Bring to a boil, then reduce the heat to medium and cook until thickened, about 5 minutes, whisking occasionally.

Remove the pan from the heat and stir in the cheeses until fully melted. Add the cooked macaroni and heat over medium heat, stirring constantly, until steaming and heated through, about 5 minutes.

Pour the macaroni mixture into the prepared baking dish. Sprinkle the bacon evenly over the top, then top with the breadcrumbs.

Broil until the breadcrumbs are toasted, 3 to 4 minutes. Remove from the broiler, let sit for 5 minutes, then serve.

DEBBIE'S GRANDKIDS' ROLLS

Makes 18

I make this with the grandkids, and it's always a hit. Not only is it delicious, it's a great way to have fun in the kitchen with kids of any age. Jazmine, our oldest grandchild, helped with these when she was two years old. Every grandchild has dipped these rolls at one time or another.

Preheat the oven to 350°F. Grease a Bundt pan.

In a small bowl, mix the melted butter and salt. Pour the cheese into another small bowl.

Roll each frozen roll in the melted butter, then the cheese to completely coat it. Place it in the Bundt pan. Repeat with the remaining rolls, stacking them evenly around the ring.

Bake for 40 to 45 minutes, until the rolls are puffed and golden brown. Cool the pan on a cooling rack for 5 minutes, then invert the pan onto a serving plate. Pull apart and enjoy the rolls warm.

4 tablespoons (½ stick) butter, melted

¼ teaspoon salt

1½ cups finely grated Parmesan cheese

18 frozen bake-and-serve dinner rolls, such as Rhodes brand

You can double this recipe.

NO-KNEAD DUTCH OVEN BREAD

Makes 1 loaf

This crusty loaf takes less than ten minutes of hands-on time. You can't beat that! Instead of kneading, you let time and yeast do the work. The end product is a bakery-worthy homemade bread.

3 cups flour, plus more for dusting
½ teaspoon active dry yeast
1¼ teaspoons salt
1½ cups hot (110°F) tap water

In a large bowl, whisk together the flour, yeast, and salt. Add the hot water and stir to combine. Cover with plastic wrap and let the mixture sit at room temperature for 3 hours, or until the dough has doubled in size and is full of bubbles.

Scrape the dough onto a floured surface and sprinkle more flour on top. Use a bench scraper to fold the dough on itself on each side, ten times total, and form into a loose ball. Transfer the dough to a piece of parchment paper, then transfer both to a clean bowl. Cover with plastic wrap and let sit for 35 to 40 minutes.

Place a Dutch oven covered with its lid in a cold oven, then preheat the oven to 450°F.

When the oven temperature has reached 450°F, use hot pads to remove the Dutch oven. Remove the lid and carefully transfer both the parchment paper and the dough to the Dutch oven. Replace the lid and return the pan to the oven.

Bake for 30 minutes, then remove the lid and slide the parchment paper out. Bake the bread for 10 more minutes, or until the crust is golden and the loaf sounds hollow when tapped.

Turn the loaf onto a wire rack and cool completely before slicing.

DESSERTS

My granddaughter Jazmine and I took a series of cake decorating classes a few years back. We had a great time. For the final class, we each decorated an elaborate cake, which I immediately took home and placed inside the freezer before anyone could take a bite. The way I looked at it, it was my masterpiece and no one dared to ruin its perfection. Jazmine shared her beautifully crafted cake with her family right away, but not me. Stay away from my creation! The sad end to this story is that a year later I discovered my neglected jewel of a cake hidden in the back of the freezer and was forced to toss it. I should have shared it when I had the chance, for all to enjoy.

This made me think of a Facebook post I recently saw: *The more you weigh, the harder you are to kidnap. Stay safe. Eat cake.* I'm taking that advice to heart. I encourage you to do the same. Create, share, and *eat* dessert. My dear aunt Betty lived to be 105, and she ate dessert every day! I remember joining her for breakfast one time, and she served homemade coconut cream pie. She was my kind of woman. You only live once—you might as well enjoy dessert.

COOKIES AND CREAM FROZEN DESSERT

Serves 24

This is a fun and easy recipe that is sure to please the entire family, especially the kids. Other than homemade cookies, Oreos are Wayne's favorite, especially the vanilla ones. I originally made this with chocolate cookies, but it's equally delicious with the vanilla version.

Make the crust:

In a large bowl, combine the crushed cookies and melted butter. Spread evenly over a 9 x 13-inch baking pan. Place the pan in the freezer until hard and cold, about 30 minutes.

Spread the ice cream evenly over the crust. Freeze until hard, about 1 hour.

Make the fudge:

In a medium saucepan over medium-high heat, bring the chocolate, butter, evaporated milk, and sugar to a boil, stirring constantly to melt the chocolate. Reduce the heat to medium-low and simmer for 2 to 3 minutes, until thickened. Remove the pan from the heat and stir in the vanilla. Let cool completely.

Remove the baking pan from the freezer and spread the fudge over the ice cream. Freeze for 30 minutes.

Make the whipped cream:

Pour the cream and powdered sugar into a large bowl. Use an electric hand mixer on high to whip the mixture until soft peaks form.

Remove the baking pan from the freezer. Spread the whipped cream evenly on top of the fudge. Cover with plastic wrap and freeze for at least 2 hours before serving.

To serve, remove the pan from the freezer and let stand at room temperature for 10 minutes. Uncover, cut into pieces, and serve immediately.

Crust:
1 (16-ounce) package chocolate sandwich cookies, such as Oreos, crushed
½ cup (1 stick) butter, melted

½ gallon vanilla ice cream, softened

Fudge:
4 ounces unsweetened chocolate, chopped
2 tablespoons butter
1 (12-ounce) can evaporated milk
1 cup sugar
1 teaspoon vanilla extract

Whipped cream:
1½ cups cream
¼ cup powdered sugar

This dessert can be made up to 1 week in advance and stored, tightly covered with plastic wrap, in the freezer. (Though I've never had it last that long!) If you're not serving a crowd, it can easily be halved and made in an 8 x 8-inch square pan.

LAURIE'S COOKIE "SALAD"

Serves 8 to 10

Family fights have been known to break out when it comes to who gets the leftovers of my daughter-in-law Laurie's contributions! This cookie "salad" is really a dessert, and so good you'll want to make a second batch to squirrel away for yourself. Sweet and creamy, it is perfect for a buffet table. When grandsons Jaxon and Collin come to visit, they like to bring this treat with them to share with the rest of the family.

1 cup buttermilk

1 (3.4-ounce) box instant vanilla pudding

1 (8-ounce) container Cool Whip, thawed

1 (8-ounce) can crushed pineapple with juice

2 bananas, sliced into ½-inch rounds

½ package Keebler Original Fudge Stripes Cookies, crushed, plus more for garnish

In a large bowl, whisk together the buttermilk and pudding mix until thick. Fold in the Cool Whip. Stir in the pineapple, bananas, and crushed cookies. Sprinkle extra crushed cookies on top, if desired.

This can be made up to 4 hours before serving. You don't need to keep it refrigerated, but it's best eaten the day it's made.

CANNOLI ICEBOX CAKE

Serves 12 to 14

This icebox cake goes beyond the classic whipped cream and chocolate wafer combination (that is always simply delicious!). The creamy, melt-in-your-mouth filling resembles cannoli filling and gets sandwiched between graham crackers. The layers all meld into one delicious dessert that is sure to tempt family and friends.

In a large bowl, beat the cream and ¼ cup of the powdered sugar with an electric hand mixer on high speed until soft peaks form.

In a separate large bowl, beat the mascarpone with the remaining 1½ cups powdered sugar, the cinnamon, and vanilla with an electric hand mixer on medium speed until smooth and completely blended. Gently fold in 3 cups of the whipped cream.

Cover the bottom of a 9 x 13-inch pan with one sleeve (9 crackers) of graham crackers, breaking up some to fit. Spread half of the filling on top, then top with another layer of graham crackers. Spread the rest of the filling on top, then lay on a final layer of graham crackers.

Spread the reserved whipped cream evenly on top and sprinkle with the mini chocolate chips. Cover with plastic wrap and refrigerate for at least 6 hours or overnight. Cut into squares and serve cold.

2½ cups cream

1¾ cups powdered sugar

32 ounces mascarpone cheese

½ teaspoon ground cinnamon

1 teaspoon vanilla extract

1 (14.4-ounce) box graham crackers

½ cup mini chocolate chips

You can also make this with a mix of 16 ounces mascarpone cheese and 16 ounces whole milk ricotta. It's not quite as rich but just as delicious.

CHOCOLATE PEPPERMINT TRIFLE

Serves 10 to 12

Trifle is one of my favorite desserts. One year for Christmas, my wonderful staff got me my very own trifle bowl. You can also make it in individual glass or plastic glasses.

Make the pudding according to the instructions on the box. While the pudding is still hot, add the white chocolate chips and peppermint extract and stir until the chips are melted and the mixture is smooth. Place plastic wrap directly on the surface of the pudding so that a skin does not form. Cool completely in the refrigerator.

When you're ready to assemble the trifle, in a large bowl, whip the cream with an electric hand mixer on high speed just until stiff peaks form.

Place a layer of half of the brownie cubes in a large glass bowl, followed by half of the peppermint white chocolate pudding, then half of the whipped cream. Repeat with one more layer of brownies, pudding, and whipped cream. Sprinkle the top with the crushed peppermint candies. Spoon into bowls and serve.

1 (4.6-ounce) box cook and serve vanilla pudding

1½ cups white chocolate chips

⅜ teaspoon peppermint extract

2 cups cream

1 (8 x 8-inch) pan of brownies, cut into small cubes

5 hard peppermint candies, crushed

This can be served immediately, or assembled and stored, covered, in the refrigerator for up to 2 hours before serving.

CARAMEL APPLE UPSIDE-DOWN CAKE

Serves 8 to 10

I don't think I need to say anything about this dessert other than "Someone, please—hand me a fork!"

Caramel apple topping:
2 tablespoons butter
⅓ cup brown sugar
3 tablespoons light corn syrup
Pinch of salt
3 Granny Smith apples, peeled, cored, and thinly sliced

Cake:
1½ cups flour
1 teaspoon baking powder
¼ teaspoon salt
1 teaspoon ground cinnamon
⅛ teaspoon ground nutmeg
½ cup (1 stick) butter
⅓ cup granulated sugar
⅓ cup brown sugar
2 eggs
1 teaspoon vanilla extract
½ cup milk
Ice cream or whipped cream, for serving

Preheat the oven to 350°F.

Make the caramel apple topping:

In a small saucepan, combine the butter, brown sugar, corn syrup, and salt and heat over medium heat, stirring occasionally, until the brown sugar is dissolved. Pour into an 8-inch round cake pan and spread evenly.

Beginning at the outer edge of the pan and working inward, lay the apple slices in concentric circles, overlapping the slices.

Make the cake:

In a medium bowl, whisk together the flour, baking powder, salt, cinnamon, and nutmeg.

In a large bowl, beat the butter with an electric hand mixer on high speed until fluffy, then add the granulated sugar and brown sugar and beat until well mixed. Add the eggs one at a time, mixing well after each addition.

Add half of the flour mixture and stir with a spatula just until incorporated. Add the vanilla and milk and stir until incorporated. Add the last of the flour mixture and stir until incorporated. Pour the batter on top of the caramel apples and smooth with a spatula.

Bake for 35 to 40 minutes, until a knife inserted in the center comes out clean. Let the cake cool in the pan for 10 minutes.

Run a knife around the edge of the pan, then invert the cake onto a plate. Serve warm, topped with ice cream or whipped cream.

BOSTON CREAM PIE POKE CAKE

Serves 8 to 10

Our daughter, Jody, is a recipe collector like my mom and me. Her Facebook page is filled with one recipe after another. She's willing to try just about anything, especially desserts.

A classic Boston cream pie is a yellow cake layered with custard and covered with a chocolate glaze. This poke version gives you all those flavors in any easy-to-transport-and-serve sheet cake. It can be made a day ahead.

Cake:
3 cups cake flour
1 tablespoon baking powder
1 teaspoon baking soda
¾ teaspoon salt
¾ cup (1½ sticks) butter, at room temperature
1½ cups sugar
3 eggs
2 teaspoons vanilla extract
1½ cups milk

Filling:
2 (3.4-ounce) boxes cook and serve vanilla pudding
4 cups milk

Glaze:
4 ounces unsweetened chocolate, chopped
6 tablespoons (¾ stick) butter, cubed
¼ cup cream
1¼ cups powdered sugar, sifted
½ teaspoon vanilla extract

Preheat the oven to 350°F. Grease a 9 x 13-inch baking pan.

Make the cake:

In a small bowl, whisk together the cake flour, baking powder, baking soda, and salt.

In a large bowl, beat the butter and sugar with an electric hand mixer on high speed until light and fluffy. Add the eggs one at a time, mixing well between additions. Mix in the vanilla. Alternately add the flour mixture and milk, starting and ending with the flour, mixing just until combined between each addition. Scrape the batter into the prepared pan and smooth the top.

Bake for 30 to 35 minutes, until a toothpick inserted in the center comes out clean.

Make the filling:

While cake is baking, cook the pudding with the milk according to the directions on the package.

Remove the cake from the oven, and while it is still hot, poke holes all over the cake with the handle of a wooden spoon, making sure to push all the way to the bottom of the pan. Pour the hot pudding onto the hot cake. Use a rubber spatula to spread the pudding evenly over the cake while gently pushing it into the holes. Cover the pan with plastic wrap and place it in the refrigerator for at least 30 minutes.

Make the glaze:

In a medium saucepan, melt the chocolate and butter over medium heat, stirring occasionally. Remove from the heat and whisk in the cream, powdered sugar, and vanilla until smooth. Let cool for 10 minutes.

Remove the cake from the refrigerator and remove the plastic wrap. Working quickly, pour the chocolate mixture over the top of the cake and spread evenly. Cover the cake with plastic wrap and refrigerate for at least 3 hours or overnight.

Serve cold or at room temperature.

If you don't have cake flour, remove 2 tablespoons from a level cup of all-purpose flour and add 2 tablespoons of cornstarch. Whisk to combine.

WHITE CHOCOLATE CHEESECAKE WITH STRAWBERRIES

Serves 10 to 12

Fresh strawberries are the perfect tart contrast to this decadently rich cheesecake. The key to a creamy cheesecake is to have all your ingredients at room temperature. Make sure to allow at least an extra hour for everything to sit on the counter before you begin mixing. White chocolate and strawberries . . . oh, my trembling heart, be still!

1 sleeve (9 crackers) graham crackers, crushed

¼ teaspoon salt

6 tablespoons (¾ cup) butter, melted and cooled

3 (8-ounce) blocks cream cheese, at room temperature

1 cup sugar

3 eggs

½ cup sour cream

1½ teaspoons vanilla extract

10 ounces white chocolate, melted and cooled

4 cups sliced strawberries

Baking the cheesecake in the hot water bath ensures that it will cook evenly and reduces the chance that the top will crack.

Preheat the oven to 350°F. Position an oven rack in the middle position. Grease a 9-inch springform pan and place it on a large double layer of heavy-duty aluminum foil (about 18 inches square). Tightly wrap the foil around the outside of the pan to create a watertight seal.

In a medium bowl, mix the graham cracker crumbs, salt, and melted butter until well combined. Press into the bottom and 1 inch up the sides of the prepared pan. Bake for 10 to 12 minutes, until lightly browned. Remove the pan from the oven and reduce the oven temperature to 325°F.

In the bowl of a stand mixer with the paddle attachment, beat the cream cheese on medium speed for 2 minutes, or until very smooth. Add the sugar and mix well. Add the eggs, one at a time, mixing well between each addition. Add the sour cream, vanilla, and white chocolate and mix until smooth. Pour the mixture over the crust.

Set the pan in a 9 x 13-inch baking pan and place the pan on the middle rack of the oven. Fill the baking pan halfway with hot water. Bake for 50 to 60 minutes, until the cheesecake is almost set in the center. It should jiggle just a little.

Carefully remove the pan from the oven and let the cheesecake cool in the water bath for 30 minutes. Remove the pan from the water bath and let the cheesecake cool until almost at room temperature, about 2 hours. Cover and refrigerate for at least 4 hours.

Run a thin knife around the inside ring of the springform pan. Release the ring and carefully remove it. Top the cheesecake with the sliced strawberries, or serve them on the side.

LEMON CUPCAKES
WITH LEMON ZEST FROSTING

Makes 24

Lemon anything *is a favorite of my husband and our grandson Jaxon, so I was naturally drawn to this recipe. Adding the zest to the frosting gives it an extra boost of flavor.*

These are perfect for baby showers, wedding showers, bake sales, or a sweet ending to a spring-time dinner.

Make the cupcakes:

Preheat the oven to 350°F. Line two 12-cup muffin tins with paper liners.

In a medium bowl, whisk together the flour, baking powder, baking soda, and salt.

In a large bowl, beat the butter and sugar together with an electric hand mixer until light and fluffy. Add the eggs, one at a time, beating well after each addition. Add the lemon zest and lemon juice and mix to combine. With the mixer on low speed, alternately add the flour mixture and buttermilk to the bowl, beginning and ending with the flour and mixing just until combined after each addition. Do not overbeat.

Scoop the batter into the cupcake liners, filling each two-thirds full. Bake for 22 to 25 minutes, until a toothpick inserted in the center of a cupcake comes out clean. Let the cupcakes cool in the pans for 5 minutes, then remove to a cooling rack to cool completely.

Make the buttercream:

In a large bowl, beat the butter with an electric hand mixer on medium speed until smooth. Reduce the speed to low, add 1½ cups of the powdered sugar, and mix until smooth. Add the cream, lemon zest, and lemon juice and mix to combine. Add the remaining 1½ cups powdered

Cupcakes:
1¼ cups flour
¾ teaspoon baking powder
¼ teaspoon baking soda
⅛ teaspoon salt
½ cup (1 stick) butter, at room temperature
1 cup sugar
2 eggs
1½ teaspoons lemon zest
1 tablespoon lemon juice
½ cup buttermilk

Buttercream:
½ cup (1 stick) butter, at room temperature
3 cups powdered sugar, sifted
2 tablespoons cream
2 teaspoons lemon zest
2 tablespoons plus 1 teaspoon lemon juice

Garnish:
1 tablespoon lemon zest
1 tablespoon sugar

sugar. When the sugar is incorporated, raise the mixer speed and mix until light and fluffy.

Make the garnish:

In a small bowl, toss the lemon zest and sugar together.

Frost the cooled cupcakes and sprinkle with the sugared lemon zest.

Using an ice cream scoop makes filling the cupcake liners easy. The frosting can be piped or spread on the cupcakes.

ALMOND BISCOTTI

Makes 32

These crispy cookies are perfect for dipping in coffee, tea, or hot chocolate. They are also delicious dipped in or drizzled with melted chocolate. They make a wonderful gift. Renate Roth was my assistant for twenty-two years. She baked these for me every year for my birthday.

Preheat the oven to 325°F. Line two rimmed baking sheets with parchment paper.

In a medium bowl, whisk together the flour, baking powder, baking soda, and salt.

In a large bowl, cream the butter and sugar with an electric hand mixer on high speed until light and fluffy. Add the eggs, one at a time, mixing well between additions. Mix in the vanilla and almond extracts. Add the flour mixture and mix until just combined. Fold in the almonds.

Divide the dough into thirds. On one of the baking sheets, shape each third into a log that's 10 inches long by 2 inches wide, leaving equal space between each log.

Bake for 25 to 30 minutes, until the logs have puffed and spread out to touch each other. Remove the baking sheet from the oven and cool on a cooling rack for 10 minutes.

Reduce the oven temperature to 275°F.

Remove one log at a time to a cutting board and slice the dough on a diagonal into ¾-inch slices. Place the cookies on the baking sheets cut-side down.

Bake for 15 minutes, flip the cookies, and bake for 15 more minutes, until the biscotti are brittle and light golden brown on both sides. Remove the biscotti to a cooling rack and let them cool completely.

2¼ cups flour

1 teaspoon baking powder

½ teaspoon baking soda

½ teaspoon salt

½ cup (1 stick) butter, at room temperature

1 cup sugar

3 eggs

1 teaspoon vanilla extract

1 teaspoon almond extract

1 cup toasted chopped almonds

The biscotti will keep for up to 2 weeks in an airtight container at room temperature or up to 3 months in the freezer.

CHOCOLATE ESPRESSO COOKIES

Makes 18

Espresso powder enhances the deep, dark chocolate flavor of these chewy, fudgy, generously sized cookies. Oh so-o-o good!

1 cup flour

½ cup unsweetened cocoa powder

2 teaspoons instant espresso powder

1 teaspoon baking soda

¾ teaspoon salt

½ cup (1 stick) butter, at room temperature

½ cup granulated sugar

½ cup brown sugar

1 egg

1½ teaspoons vanilla extract

⅓ cup semisweet chocolate chips

Preheat the oven to 350°F. Line two rimmed baking sheets with parchment paper.

Sift the flour, cocoa powder, espresso powder, baking soda, and salt into a medium bowl.

In a large bowl, cream together the butter, granulated sugar, and brown sugar with an electric hand mixer on high speed until light and fluffy. Add the egg and vanilla and mix well. With the mixer on low speed, slowly add the flour mixture and mix just until blended. Stir in the chocolate chips by hand.

Scoop out 2 tablespoons of the dough and roll into a ball. Repeat with the rest of the dough, spacing the cookies evenly on the prepared baking sheets. Bake for 9 to 11 minutes. Do not overbake; the cookies will look underdone. It's better to underbake and have a fudgy cookie than overbake and have a dry one. Let cool completely on the cookie sheets.

You can use natural or Dutch-process cocoa in this recipe; either will give you a delicious result.

The cookies can be stored at room temperature in an airtight container for up to 4 days.

CHOCOLATE THUMBPRINTS
WITH SALTED CARAMEL FILLING

Makes 20

Filled with gooey salted caramel, these dense chocolate thumbprints are hard to stop eating! The grandkids enjoy putting their own mark in these cookies.

The caramel filling isn't fussy, and it stays soft. You'll probably have some left over when you're done filling the cookies. Warmed gently, it's delicious over ice cream.

Cookies:
1 cup flour
½ cup unsweetened cocoa powder
¼ teaspoon salt
½ cup (1 stick) butter, at room temperature
⅔ cup sugar
1 egg
1 teaspoon vanilla extract

Salted caramel:
1 cup sugar
6 tablespoons (¾ cup) butter, cubed
1 teaspoon salt
½ teaspoon vanilla extract
½ cup cream

Make the cookies:

In a medium bowl, whisk together the flour, cocoa powder, and salt.

In a large bowl, beat the butter and sugar with an electric hand mixer until light and fluffy. Beat in the egg and vanilla until completely combined. With the mixer on low, gradually mix in the flour mixture until just combined. Cover the bowl and refrigerate for 15 minutes.

Make the salted caramel:

In a medium saucepan, melt the sugar over medium-high heat, stirring occasionally with a heatproof rubber spatula. When the sugar is melted and has turned a deep amber color, after 6 to 7 minutes, carefully whisk in the butter and salt. When the butter has melted, add the vanilla and cream. Be careful, as the mixture may bubble up and splatter. Remove from the heat and let cool. It will stay soft.

Preheat the oven to 350°F. Line a rimmed baking sheet with aluminum foil or parchment paper.

Scoop 1 tablespoon of the dough and roll it into a ball. Place on the prepared baking sheet and press a deep indentation into the center of the cookie with your thumb. If the dough is sticky, dip your finger in sugar before pressing. Repeat until all the dough is used. These cookies don't spread, so you can leave as little as an inch between them.

Bake the cookies for 8 to 10 minutes, until set. Remove them from the oven and carefully transfer the parchment paper with the cookies to a cooling rack. Let cool for at least 10 minutes.

Fill the center of each cookie with 1 teaspoon caramel.

Store the cookies at room temperature or in the refrigerator in an airtight container stacked between layers of wax paper. Or freeze in a single layer, then place in an airtight container and freeze for up to 3 months.

Any extra caramel will keep covered in the refrigerator for up to 1 month.

You can use Dutch-process or natural cocoa powder here.

SKILLET COOKIE

Serves 6

Here's the ultimate family dinner dessert. This cookie is served warm: gooey on the inside and crispy at the edges. Topped with scoops of ice cream, it's meant to be shared.

For optimum lusciousness, it's better to underbake than overbake the cookie. It will continue to bake in the pan.

Leftovers will keep for a day (or maybe two) tightly covered with aluminum foil at room temperature, but it won't be as decadently yummy as it is right out of the oven.

Preheat the oven to 350°F.

In a medium bowl, whisk together the flour, baking powder, baking soda, and salt.

In a large bowl, cream the butter, granulated sugar, and brown sugar with an electric hand mixer on high speed until light and fluffy. Add the egg and vanilla and mix on low speed until incorporated. Add the flour mixture and mix just until combined. Do not overmix or the cookie will be tough. Stir in the mix-ins by hand. The batter will be very thick.

Pour the batter into a 10-inch cast-iron skillet or 9-inch round cake pan and use your hands to spread it evenly.

Bake for 27 to 30 minutes in the skillet or 25 to 27 minutes in the cake pan, until golden brown and crispy at the edges. Remove from the oven and let cool for 5 minutes.

Serve hot or warm with scoops of ice cream in the middle and spoons for sharing.

Don't use a baking pan larger than 10 inches or the cookie will be dry; it's better to use a smaller, deeper pan than a broad, shallow one.

1½ cups flour

¾ teaspoon baking powder

½ teaspoon baking soda

¼ teaspoon salt

½ cup (1 stick) butter, at room temperature

½ cup granulated sugar

½ cup brown sugar

1 egg

1 teaspoon vanilla extract

1 cup mix-ins (see below)

Your favorite ice cream, for serving

Suggested mix-ins:

½ cup white chocolate chips, plus ½ cup salted macadamia nuts

½ cup dried cranberries, plus ½ cup toasted chopped cashews

½ cup semisweet chocolate chips, plus ½ cup walnuts

½ cup chopped toffee bits, plus ½ cup chopped hazelnuts

½ cup shredded coconut, plus ½ cup semisweet chocolate chips

EGGNOG COOKIES

Makes 32

These cookies melt in your mouth. The eggnog flavor is deliciously baked into a buttery cookie and gives richness to the frosting. It's a perfect winter holiday treat. These are the cookies Merry baked for Jayson in Merry and Bright.

Cookies:
2¼ cups flour
2 teaspoons baking powder
½ teaspoon salt
½ teaspoon ground cinnamon
½ teaspoon ground nutmeg
¾ cup (1½ sticks) butter, at room temperature
½ cup granulated sugar
½ cup light brown sugar
2 egg yolks
1 teaspoon vanilla extract
½ teaspoon rum extract
½ cup eggnog

Frosting:
½ cup (1 stick) butter, at room temperature
¼ teaspoon salt
1 tablespoon eggnog
½ teaspoon rum extract
3 cups powdered sugar
⅛ teaspoon ground nutmeg, for sprinkling

These can be stored in an airtight container at room temperature, with layers separated by parchment or wax paper, for up to 3 days.

Make the cookies:

Preheat the oven to 350°F. Line two rimmed baking sheets with parchment paper.

In a medium bowl, whisk together the flour, baking powder, salt, cinnamon, and nutmeg.

In a large bowl, cream together the butter, granulated sugar, and brown sugar with an electric hand mixer on high speed until light and fluffy. Add the egg yolks and mix just until combined. Mix in the vanilla, rum extract, and eggnog. Slowly mix in the dry ingredients just until combined.

Scoop the dough by heaping tablespoonful onto the prepared baking sheets, spacing them 2 inches apart. Bake for 11 to 13 minutes, until very light golden brown. Allow the cookies to rest on the baking sheets for 2 to 3 minutes before transferring to wire racks to cool completely.

Make the frosting:

In a large bowl, cream the butter with an electric hand mixer on high speed until very light and fluffy. Mix in the salt, eggnog, and rum extract. Sift in the powdered sugar 1 cup at a time, mixing well between additions. Spread onto the cooled cookies and sprinkle with the nutmeg.

WAYNE'S WHISKEY BACON BROWNIES

Makes 9 squares

Brownies are a favorite of both my husband and my boys. Ted and Dale would often eat an entire batch, hot from the oven, before their dad had a chance to get a single square. The brown sugar–whiskey buttercream frosting takes these right over the top.

Preheat the oven to 350°F. Line the bottom and sides of an 8 x 8-inch baking pan with two rectangles of parchment paper, leaving a 2-inch overhang on all sides.

Make the brownies:

In a small saucepan, melt the butter and chocolate over medium heat, stirring constantly. Remove the pan from the heat and let cool for 10 minutes.

Transfer the chocolate to a large bowl and stir in the sugar. Add the eggs one at a time, stirring well to combine between each addition. Add the flour and salt and stir just until combined. Stir in the vanilla and whiskey. Pour the batter into the prepared pan and smooth the top.

Bake for 40 to 45 minutes, until a knife inserted in the center has just a few crumbs attached. Set the pan on a wire rack to cool.

Make the buttercream frosting:

In a large bowl, beat the butter with an electric hand mixer on high speed until light and fluffy. Add the brown sugar and beat until fluffy. Add 1 cup of the powdered sugar and mix until incorporated. Add the whiskey and vanilla and mix until all incorporated. Add the remaining 1 cup powdered sugar and the salt and mix until well combined.

Spread the buttercream on the cooled brownies, then sprinkle the bacon on top. Cut into squares and serve.

Brownies:
½ cup (1 stick) butter
8 ounces bittersweet chocolate, chopped
1½ cups sugar
4 eggs
¾ cup flour
¾ teaspoon salt
1 teaspoon vanilla extract
1½ tablespoons whiskey

Buttercream frosting:
½ cup (1 stick) butter, at room temperature
¼ cup brown sugar
2 cups powdered sugar, sifted
1½ tablespoons whiskey
1 teaspoon vanilla extract
⅛ teaspoon salt
8 slices bacon, cooked, drained, and crumbled

These will keep for 2 days at room temperature, covered in plastic wrap or aluminum foil, if they last that long.

LEMON SHORTBREAD BARS WITH STREUSEL TOPPING

Makes 32

This may not be what comes to mind when you think of a traditional lemon bar. I think they're better. These are a sure hit at all of my family gatherings.

Crust:
2 cups flour
3 tablespoons sugar
¼ teaspoon salt
¾ cup (1½ sticks) cold butter, cut into pieces
2 egg yolks

Filling:
6 eggs
2 cups sugar
5 teaspoons lemon zest
⅔ cup lemon juice
½ cup flour

Streusel:
¾ cup flour
½ cup sugar
1 teaspoon baking powder
¼ teaspoon salt
4 tablespoons (½ stick) cold butter, cut into ½-inch pieces
Powdered sugar, for garnish

These will keep, tightly covered, in the refrigerator for 4 to 5 days.

Preheat the oven to 350°F. Grease a 9 x 13-inch baking pan and line the bottom with parchment paper.

Make the crust:

Combine the flour, sugar, salt, and butter in a food processor and pulse until the mixture resembles coarse meal. Add the egg yolks and process just until the mixture forms clumps. Press the mixture onto the bottom of the prepared pan.

Bake just until the edges are golden brown, 16 to 18 minutes. Remove from the oven and reduce the temperature to 325°F.

Make the filling:

In a large bowl, whisk together the eggs, sugar, lemon zest, and lemon juice until combined. Add the flour and whisk until blended. Pour over the hot shortbread crust and bake until the filling is set, 20 to 25 minutes.

Make the streusel:

In a medium bowl, combine the flour, sugar, baking powder, and salt. Cut in the butter with a pastry blender or two forks until the mixture is crumbly. Sprinkle the streusel over the hot filling and bake until light golden, about 25 minutes.

Let cool completely, at least 1 hour. Cut into 32 bars and sprinkle with powdered sugar before serving.

CHRISTMAS FUDGE

Makes 48 pieces

In the month leading up to Christmas, my mom and I would go on a candy, cookie, and fruit-cake mission. Nearly everything we cooked or baked was intended for others. Making gifts of food is a tradition I've handed down to my own children and grandchildren. My mom loved to improvise recipes, and this variation of fudge was one of my personal favorites.

1½ cups granulated sugar
⅔ cup evaporated milk
2 tablespoons butter
¼ teaspoon salt
2⅔ cups mini-marshmallows
1½ cups semisweet chocolate chips
1 teaspoon vanilla extract

The fudge will keep for up to 2 weeks in an airtight container at room temperature, or tightly wrapped in aluminum foil or plastic wrap in the refrigerator for up to 1 month.

Line the bottom and sides of an 8 x 8-inch square baking pan with two pieces of aluminum foil, leaving a 2-inch overhang on all sides.

In a large, heavy-bottomed saucepan, combine the sugar, evaporated milk, butter, and salt. Bring the mixture to a rolling boil over medium-high heat and boil for 5 minutes, stirring constantly.

Remove the pan from the heat and immediately add 2 cups of the marshmallows, the chocolate chips, and vanilla. Stir until the marshmallows and chocolate chips are melted and the mixture is completely smooth. Stir the remaining marshmallows into the fudge until just combined but not melted. You want to see pieces of marshmallow. Pour the fudge into the prepared baking pan.

Refrigerate the fudge for at least 2 hours, until set. Lift the foil from the pan and remove it from the fudge. Cut the fudge into 48 pieces.

RENELLE'S CHRISTMAS TOFFEE

Makes about 1 pound

My friend Renelle gave me this recipe a few years back. While I call it Christmas toffee, this recipe is good any time of the year. It's simple, easy, and so delectable that it will disappear faster than ice cream on the hottest day of the year.

Line a rimmed baking sheet with aluminum foil or parchment paper.

In a medium saucepan, combine the butter, sugar, and ¼ teaspoon of the salt and melt over medium-high heat. Bring to a boil, then boil for about 10 minutes, stirring constantly, until the mixture is a medium brown color and reaches 290°F on an instant-read thermometer. Pour the mixture onto the prepared baking sheet and quickly spread to the edges of the pan. Let sit for 2 to 3 minutes to set, then sprinkle the chocolate chips evenly over the top. Let the chocolate sit for 2 to 3 minutes, then spread it evenly over the toffee. Sprinkle with the remaining ¼ teaspoon salt.

Place the pan in the refrigerator until the chocolate is set, 10 to 15 minutes. Break into pieces and serve.

1 cup (2 sticks) butter
1 cup sugar
½ teaspoon salt
1 cup semisweet chocolate chips

The toffee is best stored in the refrigerator in an airtight container, where it will keep for up to a week, but it can be stored at room temperature for up to 3 days.

WHITE CHOCOLATE BARK

Makes about 1½ pounds

I love white chocolate in any form! You can customize this candy bark with any combination of fruits, nuts, and candies that strikes your fancy. Use your imagination and think outside the box! It makes an easy but impressive gift or party favor.

Line a rimmed baking sheet with aluminum foil or parchment paper.

Put the white chocolate in a microwave-safe bowl. Microwave on high in 30-second increments, stirring in between, until almost melted, 1 to 2 minutes. Stir until completely melted and smooth.

Pour the white chocolate onto the prepared baking sheet and spread it into a rectangle about 10 x 12 inches and ¼ inch thick. Sprinkle the toppings evenly over the white chocolate, pressing them in lightly.

Refrigerate the bark on the baking sheet until hardened, about 30 minutes. Peel off the foil or parchment paper and cut or break into pieces.

1 pound white chocolate, chopped

Suggested mix-ins:
½ cup dried cranberries, plus ⅓ cup shelled pistachios, coarsely chopped
½ cup M&M's, plus 1 cup mini or small pretzels
¼ cup dried blueberries, plus ¼ cup chopped dried cherries, plus ½ cup chopped toasted almonds
½ cup chopped dried apricots, plus ½ cup chopped salted, roasted cashews

Store this in an airtight container in the refrigerator for up to a week.

MARIONBERRY PIE

Serves 6 to 8

Marionberries are a kind of blackberry developed and grown in Oregon. Almost all of them are devoured locally (lucky us!). If you can't find marionberries, any fresh blackberry will make a delicious pie!

Make the crust:

In a large bowl, whisk together the flour, sugar, and salt. With a pastry cutter or two knives, cut in the butter until the mixture resembles coarse meal. Drizzle the water over the mixture and use your hands to mix lightly. The dough should be slightly crumbly but hold together when squeezed with your hand. Add up to 1 tablespoon more water if you need to.

Cut the dough into two pieces and place each piece on a piece of plastic wrap. Place another piece of plastic wrap on top of each piece of dough and push each piece into a circle about ½ inch thick. Wrap tightly and place in the refrigerator for at least 1 hour or overnight.

Preheat the oven to 375°F. Line a rimmed baking sheet with aluminum foil.

On a floured surface, roll out each piece of dough into a 13-inch circle. Place one piece inside a 9-inch pie plate. Trim the overhang with a knife.

Make the filling:

In a large bowl, toss the marionberries with the sugar, flour, and lemon juice. Pour the berries into the piecrust and dot with the butter. Place the second piece of dough on top. Fold the overhang under itself and crimp the edges decoratively. Cut four slits in the top with a sharp knife. Place the pie on the prepared baking sheet.

Bake the pie for 60 to 70 minutes, until the crust is

Crust:
- 2½ cups flour, plus additional for dusting
- 1 teaspoon sugar
- 1 teaspoon salt
- 1 cup (2 sticks) cold butter, cut into cubes
- ¼ cup ice water, plus up to 1 tablespoon more if needed

Filling:
- 5 cups fresh marionberries, rinsed
- ½ cup sugar
- 4 tablespoons flour
- 2 teaspoons lemon juice
- 1 tablespoon cold butter, cut into cubes

golden brown and the filling is bubbling. Remove the pie from the oven and let cool at room temperature for at least 1 hour. Slice and serve warm or at room temperature.

This will keep, covered in plastic wrap or aluminum foil, at room temperature for 2 days.

DECADENT DARK CHOCOLATE SALTED CARAMEL TART

Serves 10 to 12

Trying to wow your guests? This tart will do it.

Make the crust:

In a food processor, pulse the cookies until finely crushed. Add the melted butter and pulse until completely combined. Press the crumb mixture into the bottom and up the sides of a 10-inch tart pan with a removable bottom. Refrigerate the crust for at least 15 minutes.

Make the filling:

In a small saucepan, combine the brown sugar and butter. Cook over medium heat, whisking constantly, until it begins to boil. Continue cooking and whisking for 1 minute. Remove the pan from the heat and whisk in the cream until incorporated and smooth. Cool the caramel for 15 minutes, then pour it over the crust, spreading it evenly. Refrigerate the tart for about 30 minutes, until set.

Make the glaze:

Place the chocolate chips in a medium heatproof bowl. In a small saucepan, bring the cream to a simmer over medium-high heat. Pour the hot cream over the chocolate chips and let sit for 5 minutes. Whisk until completely smooth, then pour the melted chocolate over the caramel and smooth with a rubber spatula. Refrigerate for about 30 minutes, until chilled and set.

Sprinkle the top evenly with the fleur de sel. Serve chilled.

Crust:
1 (14.3-ounce) package chocolate sandwich cookies, such as Oreos
½ cup (1 stick) butter, melted

Filling:
⅔ cup packed light brown sugar
½ cup (1 stick) butter
¼ cup cream

Glaze:
12 ounces dark chocolate chips
1 cup cream
1 tablespoon fleur de sel or salt

Once it's set, you can cover the tart and keep it for up to 2 days in the refrigerator.

DRINKS

I'll never forget my first taste of champagne. It was a bottle we inherited from Wayne's mother, Marie, and prior to that, it was a gift from her longtime friend Cy Higginbotham. Wayne's father had died from a war injury when Wayne was young, and Marie had never remarried. However, Marie dated Cy for years, and when he died childless, he left most of his estate to Marie. Among his possessions were a few bottles of expensive wine and champagne.

Because Marie never drank any alcohol, she decided to give Wayne this special bottle of champagne with the instruction "Be sure to open this to celebrate when Debbie sells her first book." At that point, I was already five years into my long sojourn of sending manuscripts to publishers, and it felt like a pipe dream. I feared that the beautiful bottle of champagne would be worth a *whole* lot of money by the time New York finally accepted one of my stories! Little did I know, I would make that first unforgettable sale within a few short months after we had carefully stored the champagne for safekeeping. I've tasted a lot of champagne in the years since, but none is as memorable as the bottle from Cy that Wayne and I used to toast the beginning of my writing career.

Once our children were grown and out of the house, Wayne and I became interested in collecting wine. Our first trip to the California wine country is what started it all. I surprised Wayne with a trip to Napa and Sonoma for his birthday, and had arranged a hot-air balloon ride along with a wine tour. We purchased our first case of wine that weekend, and we've never looked back. We rarely find the need to visit California for wine any longer, because Washington State's wine production has grown to the point that we have more than enough wineries in our own state to tour, to taste, and to buy wine. Seven years ago we built a wine cellar in our home, which we are both extremely proud to show to family and friends.

When our family gathers around the table for holidays, or even at dinnertime, a special cocktail or a nice bottle of wine will always be served and enjoyed.

LAVENDER LEMONADE

This refreshing floral lemonade is a lovely shade of pink. It's the perfect drink for a brunch, baby shower, or bridal shower.

I have several lavender plants in my yard. Over the years I've tried several ways to make use of this fragrant flower. Jo Marie from the Rose Harbor Inn series would approve of this one.

2 cups room-temperature water
1½ cups sugar
¼ cup dried culinary-grade lavender buds
1½ cups lemon juice
4 to 5 cups cold water

In a medium saucepan, combine the room-temperature water and sugar over medium-high heat. Bring to a boil, stirring occasionally to dissolve the sugar. Remove the pan from the heat and stir in the lavender. Let steep for 30 minutes.

Set a fine-mesh sieve over a medium bowl. Pour the lavender syrup into the bowl. Discard the lavender.

Pour the syrup into a pitcher. Add the lemon juice and cold water and stir to fully combine. Serve over ice.

You can keep the lemonade, in a covered container, for up to 5 days in the refrigerator. The syrup can be made up to 2 weeks ahead.

BLACKBERRY-LIME MOJITO

Makes 1 drink

Here's a refreshing cocktail perfect for a hot summer evening. Leave out the rum and you have a cooling mocktail.

Muddle the blackberries in a small bowl. Pour over a fine-mesh sieve into a tall glass. Press the berries with the back of a spoon to extract as much juice as possible. Discard the seeds.

Add the lime juice, mint leaves, and sugar to the black-berry juice. Muddle together until the mint leaves are bruised. Stir in the rum and club soda, then top with ice. Garnish with a lime slice, extra mint leaves, and a black-berry, if desired.

4 blackberries, plus additional for garnish

2 tablespoons lime juice

8 fresh mint leaves, plus additional for garnish

4 teaspoons superfine sugar

2 ounces light rum

2 ounces club soda

1 cup ice

Lime slice, for garnish

SUMMER FRUIT SANGRIA

Makes 3 to 4 quarts

There's no place on earth more beautiful than the Pacific Northwest in summer when the sun is out. Wayne and I enjoy this drink sitting on our patio during the summer months and gazing out over the beauty of Puget Sound.

In a large pitcher, stir the sugar, vodka, and brandy until the sugar is dissolved. Add the fruit and red wine and stir. Refrigerate for at least 4 hours or overnight. Add the ginger ale just before serving.

To serve, spoon some of the fruit in each glass, top with ice, and pour the sangria over the top.

¼ cup sugar

½ cup peach-flavored vodka or peach schnapps

¼ cup brandy

1 pound yellow or white peaches, nectarines, apricots, or plums, pitted and diced or thinly sliced

1 (750-milliliter) bottle red wine

1 (1-liter) bottle ginger ale

Don't spend too much on the wine for the sangria. The other ingredients will overpower any subtle flavors. A nice sturdy pinot noir, merlot, or zinfandel would be perfect.

GRAPEFRUIT FROSÉ

Serves 4 to 6

Looking for the perfect sipper for a brunch or a shower? Look no further than this sweet-tart treat. It's like a slushy for grown-ups. When our kids lived at home, the only flavor soda pop they wouldn't sneak and drink was grapefruit, which quickly became the only cans left for Wayne and me. Over the years I've grown quite fond of grapefruit anything!

2½ cups no-sugar-added grapefruit juice (not from concentrate)
¼ cup sugar
16 ounces rosé

Pour the grapefruit juice into ice cube trays and freeze until solid, about 2 hours.

In a blender, blend the frozen grapefruit juice cubes, sugar, and rosé on high speed or the ice crush setting until slushy and no big chunks of ice remain.

Pour the frosé into glasses and serve immediately.

HOMEMADE TEAS

A cup of tea can get you going in the morning, give you a break in the middle of the day, or make for a calm ending to the evening. I almost always have a tea break in the afternoon.

Packaged in an attractive jar with a pretty spoon, your own special blend of either black or herbal tea makes a lovely gift for a special friend or colleague. It's especially nice if you use herbs from your own herb garden, as I do.

You, too, can treat yourself to a cup of tea made with fresh picked leaves and blossoms. Some of the best herbs for tea are lemon balm, lemon verbena, basil, chamomile, mint, sage, lavender, and rosemary. All are easy to grow and can be used dry as well as fresh. They can be used alone or in any combination that pleases you. A good rule of thumb is one tablespoon of fresh herbs or one teaspoon of dried herbs per cup. Of course you can use more or less to taste.

Do not use herbs or flowers that have been sprayed with pesticides.

To dry herbs:

Cut your herbs during the growing season, when they are plentiful and lush. Don't wait until they are starting to wilt or have dried out from the summer heat. Cut midmorning, after the morning dew has dried from the leaves but before they are wilting in the afternoon sun.

Remove any dried or wilted leaves, and rinse the herbs with cool water. Gently shake off the excess water, then pat completely dry with paper towels. Wet herbs will mold and rot.

Bundle 4 to 6 stems together and tie into a bunch with string. Label paper bags with the name of the herb and date. Punch several holes in each bag for ventilation. Place one herb bundle upside down in each bag and gather the ends together around the stem. Tie closed with a string, leaving a long tail on the end. Hang the bags upside down in a warm, well-ventilated room. You can tie multiple bags to a hanger; a ladder works as well.

Check the herbs after 1 week. Discard any that have molded. Keep checking every few days until the herbs dry completely, when the leaves sound like crisp cornflakes when crushed.

Store in a dark, airtight container. Dried herbs will keep for about a year.

CHRISTMAS SPICE TEA

½ cup loose black tea leaves, such as Darjeeling

5 cinnamon sticks, broken up

3 tablespoons crushed dried orange peel*

2 tablespoons whole cloves

Put all the ingredients in a bowl and stir to combine. Pour into a pint mason jar and seal with the lid. Attach a decorative spoon or scoop, an infuser or small package of tea bags, and directions for brewing.

Directions:

Scoop the tea into a tea bag or a tea infuser.

For a single serving, use 1 to 2 teaspoons per 1 cup boiling water.

For a teapot, use 3 tablespoons per 4 cups boiling water.

Let steep for 5 to 7 minutes, then strain and serve.

*Peel an orange with a vegetable peeler, avoiding the white pith. Place on a cooling rack set over a rimmed baking sheet and let dry at room temperature until brittle, about 24 hours. Break into ¼-inch pieces. Store in an airtight container.

ROSY BLACK TEA

1¼ cups black tea leaves, such as Darjeeling

¾ cup dried rose petals, crumbled

Put all the ingredients in a bowl and stir to combine. Pour into a pint mason jar and seal with the lid. Attach a decorative spoon or scoop, an infuser or small package of tea bags, and directions for brewing.

Directions:

Scoop the tea into a tea bag or a tea infuser.

For a single serving, use 1 to 2 teaspoons per 1 cup boiling water.

For a teapot, use 3 tablespoons per 4 cups boiling water.

Let steep for 5 to 7 minutes, then strain and serve.

MINTY LAVENDER HERB TEA

Put all the ingredients in a bowl and stir to combine. Pour into a pint mason jar and seal with the lid. Attach a decorative spoon or scoop, an infuser or small package of tea bags, and directions for brewing.

Directions:

Scoop the tea into a tea bag or a tea infuser.

For a single serving, use 1 to 2 teaspoons per 1 cup boiling water.

For a teapot, use 3 tablespoons per 4 cups boiling water.

Let steep for 7 to 10 minutes, then strain and serve.

¾ cup dried mint leaves, crumbled

¾ cup dried lemon balm leaves, crumbled

½ cup dried lavender buds

WHITE HOT CHOCOLATE

Serves 6 to 8

Sweet, creamy, decadent, and delicious, here's a coffee-shop-worthy drink you can make in no time at home. Serve it as is to the kids, or add a splash of your favorite liquor for the adults.

In a medium saucepan, heat the milk, white chocolate, and salt over medium heat, stirring constantly, until the milk is hot and the white chocolate has melted, being careful not to let it boil. Remove the pan from the heat and stir in the vanilla.

Serve in mugs with your choice of garnishes.

6 cups milk

10 ounces white chocolate, chopped

Pinch of salt

1 teaspoon vanilla extract

Whipped cream, peppermint sticks, and/or marshmallows, for serving

MENUS

Sometimes the hardest part of putting together a meal for a special occasion is planning the menu! Here are some suggestions—some simple and some fancy—for meals I share with family and friends.

If a menu component isn't a recipe in this book, it's in italics.

DAY BEFORE THANKSGIVING FEAST

When you have grown children with spouses and significant others, holidays can mean an empty seat at the table. I've given up trying to get everyone together on Thanksgiving Day, but no one ever misses our pre-Thanksgiving dinner.

Mushroom and Caramelized Onion Bites
Standing Rib Roast
Cheddar Garlic Stuffed Potatoes
Cameron's Garlic and Bacon Green Beans
Debbie's Grandkids' Rolls
Caramel Apple Upside-Down Cake

ALL-DAY CHRISTMAS BUFFET

Rather than sitting down to a specific meal on Christmas Day, I put out a buffet so we can graze all day.

Overnight Caramel Pecan Rolls

Baked Oatmeal

Italian Herbed Popcorn

Hummus with crackers and raw vegetables

Cold cuts, sliced cheese, rolls

Broccoli Apple Cheddar Salad

Laurie's Cookie "Salad"

Chocolate Cranberry Croissant Pudding

BABY SHOWER

Lavender Lemonade

Carrot Ginger Soup

Curried Chicken Salad

Lemon Shortbread Bars with Streusel Topping

MOTHER'S DAY OR WEDDING BRUNCH

Grapefruit Frosé

Strawberries and Cream Scones with Strawberry Butter

Asparagus Tomato Quiche

Green salad

Lemon Cupcakes with Lemon Zest Frosting

FATHER'S DAY BARBECUE

Watermelon Feta Salad with Balsamic Reduction

Grilled Fish Tacos with Cilantro-Lime Sauce

Grilled Corn with Sweet and Spicy Butter

Cookies and Cream Frozen Dessert

Summer Fruit Sangria

PERFECT POTLUCK DINNER

Roasted Red Pepper Hummus

Crackers and raw vegetables

Slow Cooker Honey Garlic Chicken

Layered Beef Enchilada Casserole

Spinach-Artichoke Lasagna

Kale Caesar Salad

Boston Cream Pie Poke Cake

ELEGANT DINNER FOR SPECIAL GUESTS

Bacon-Wrapped Dates

Green salad

Herb Roasted Lamb Chops with Dijon-Rosemary Sauce

Boiled new potatoes and steamed green peas

Decadent Dark Chocolate Salted Caramel Tart

SWEET SIXTEEN/GRADUATION PARTY

Garlic Pizza Knots with Tomato Dipping Sauce

Parmesan Popcorn

Seven-Layer Dip

Chips and assorted veggies

Easy Slow Cooker Pulled Pork Nachos

White and Dark Chocolate–Drizzled Popcorn

White Chocolate Cheesecake with Strawberries

BREAKFAST FOR DINNER

Sheepherder's Skillet

Cream Cheese Danishes

White Hot Chocolate

SUMMER PICNIC

Kalamata Olive Hummus

Raw veggies

Greek Chicken Pitas with Tzatziki Sauce

Adler Potato Salad

Chocolate Espresso Cookies

LUNCH FOR FRIENDS/COMMITTEE/BUSINESS MEETING

Spicy Black Bean Soup

Crunchy Ramen Salad with Honey-Ginger Vinaigrette

Chocolate Thumbprints with Salted Caramel Filling

DEBBIE'S CHRISTMAS TEA FOR FRIENDS

Maple Pecan Scones with Bacon Maple Butter

Muffin Tin Donut Holes

Eggnog Cookies

Christmas Fudge

Almond Biscotti

White Hot Chocolate

Christmas Spice Tea

DATE NIGHT

Roasted Sesame Asparagus

Garlic Salmon Pasta in a Spicy Cream Sauce

Wayne's Whiskey Bacon Brownies

CHRISTMAS PROGRESSIVE DINNER

Warm Goat Cheese and Roasted Cherry Tomato Dip

Kale Caesar Salad

Slow Cooker Honey Garlic Chicken

Laurie's Rice

Chocolate Peppermint Trifle

SPECIAL RECIPE LISTS

GIFTS OF FOOD

Chocolate Cherry Quick Bread

Debbie's Apple Butter

Dried Soup Mixes

White Chocolate Bark

Christmas Fudge

Renelle's Christmas Toffee

Homemade Teas

WHEN YOU'RE ASKED TO BRING A DISH

Laurie's Rice

Bacon Macaroni and Cheese

Slow Cooker Honey Garlic Chicken

Debbie's Chicken and Black Bean Enchiladas

Layered Beef Enchilada Casserole

Spinach-Artichoke Lasagna

FOR FRIENDS IN NEED

Blueberry Crumb Cake

Cinnamon Streusel Coffee Coffee Cake

Overnight Caramel Pecan Rolls

Carrot Ginger Soup

Easy Slow Cooker Pulled Pork

Mozzarella-Stuffed Meatballs

Bacon Macaroni and Cheese

Debbie's Mom's Borscht

Wayne's Whiskey Bacon Brownies

Almond Biscotti

Minty Lavender Herb Tea

RECIPES FOR A CROWD

Muffin Tin Donut Holes

Pumpkin Apple Crunch Muffins

Seven-Layer Dip

Debbie's Mom's Borscht

Broccoli Apple Cheddar Salad

Laurie's Rice

Snow on the Mountain

Guinness Pot Pie

Layered Beef Enchilada Casserole

Easy Slow Cooker Pulled Pork

Spinach-Artichoke Lasagna

Laurie's Cookie "Salad"

Cookies and Cream Frozen Dessert

Cannoli Icebox Cake

Lemon Cupcakes with Lemon Zest Frosting

MAKE AHEAD/FREEZER FRIENDLY

Bacon Spinach Gouda Quiche

Chocolate Cranberry Croissant Pudding

Carrot Ginger Soup

Sausage, Kale, and Potato Soup

Easy Slow Cooker Pulled Pork

Asparagus Tomato Quiche

Guinness Pot Pie

QUICK AND EASY

Bacon-Wrapped Dates

Tomato, Egg, and Prosciutto Tarts

Roasted Sesame Asparagus

Grilled Corn with Sweet and Spicy Butter

Herb Roasted Lamb Chops with
    Dijon-Rosemary Sauce

Spicy Pork Chops

Turkey Lettuce Wraps

WHEN YOU WANT TO IMPRESS

Mushroom and Caramelized Onion Bites

Roasted Sesame Asparagus

Garlic Salmon Pasta in a Spicy Cream Sauce

Standing Rib Roast

Herb Roasted Lamb Chops with Dijon-Rosemary Sauce

Decadent Dark Chocolate Salted Caramel Tart

White Chocolate Cheesecake with Strawberries

COMPANY'S COMING—NOW

Bacon-Wrapped Dates

Sweet and Salty Nuts

Hummus

Parmesan or Italian Herbed Popcorn

Warm Goat Cheese and Roasted Cherry Tomato Dip

Skillet Cookie

TO SAY THANKS

Gratitude Bread

Almond Biscotti

Debbie's Apple Butter

Blueberry Crumb Cake

White Chocolate Bark

Renelle's Christmas Toffee

Chocolate Espresso Cookies

Homemade Teas

ACKNOWLEDGMENTS

I've always been a passionate person. I'm passionate about faith, family, and food, but even *I* am awestruck that my love of cooking and eating would become part of my writing career. That said, no book is accomplished by one person; it takes more than a village, and in this case, it required the talents of multiple people from both coasts!

Sydny Miner assembled this entire project with great professionalism and efficiency, being certain that it always had my touch on it. Thank you, Sydny. It was an honor to work with you.

Jenna Bush reconstructed the family recipes I'd never bothered to write down. I handed her a list of ingredients with instructions like: "Add zucchini and tomato juice and don't forget the garlic. Oh, and there's bacon in there too." Somehow Jenna managed to carefully reconstruct them into real recipes that make sense in every way.

Cyd McDowell and **Courtney DeWet**, our food and prop stylists—WOW!—food never looked so appealing after these two talented women worked their magic. (I need to mention that my table never looked that good, either.) All that beauty and eye appeal came to life through the camera lens of **Tina Rupp.**

Speaking of women with cameras, **Stephanie Dyane** is the photographer who took the photos of my children, grandchildren, and me. She had the patience of a saint, herding us all together. And I don't want to forget **Tim Archibald** and his crew, who took the cover photo.

A huge note of appreciation to **Shauna Summers**, my editor from Penguin Random House. I am blessed to work with her. She somehow manages to bring out the best in me. Nor can I forget **Theresa Park**, my agent from Park Literary & Media. She has given me a special gift—*her unfailing and continued belief in me*—what a difference that has made in my life and career.

And last but never least, I want to give a shout out to **Adele LaCombe**, my daughter and

CEO, as well as **Ashley Hayes**, my brand/marketing manager, both of whom worked tirelessly to keep me on task. I especially enjoyed going over my recipes with them, which spurred wonderful family memories and plenty of laughter.

I can say without reservation that a great deal of love, talent, and passion went into this project from everyone I've mentioned. Now it's your turn to read, cook, and enjoy these recipes from my heart to yours.

INDEX

(Page references in *italics* refer to illustrations.)

A

Adler Potato Salad, *120*, 121
All-Day Christmas Buffet menu, 182
almond(s):
  Biscotti, 145
  Chocolate Cranberry Croissant Pudding, 22
  Snow on the Mountain, 84
  White Chocolate Bark, *158*, 159
appetizers and snacks, 35–47
  Bacon-Wrapped Dates, 43
  Garlic Pizza Knots with Tomato Dipping Sauce, *36*, 37
  Hummus, 46
  Mushroom and Caramelized Onion Bites, 38
  Savory and Sweet Popcorn, *40*, 40–41
  Seven-Layer Dip, 47
  Sweet and Salty Nuts, 39
  Tomatillo Salsa, 42
  Warm Goat Cheese and Roasted Cherry Tomato Dip, *44*, 45
apple:
  Broccoli Cheddar Salad, *66*, 67
  Butter, Debbie's, 33
  Caramel, Upside-Down Cake, 136, *137*
  Cinnamon Baked Oatmeal, 25
  Pumpkin Crunch Muffins, 18

apricots:
  dried, in White Chocolate Bark, *158*, 159
  Summer Fruit Sangria, *168*, 169
Artichoke-Spinach Lasagne, 108
Asian flavors:
  Crunchy Ramen Salad with Honey-Ginger Vinaigrette, 68
  Peanut Butter Noodles with Thai Flavors and Crispy Tofu, *106*, 107
  Slow Cooker Honey Garlic Chicken, 75
  Turkey Lettuce Wraps, *86*, 87
asparagus:
  Roasted Sesame, 116
  Tomato Quiche, 101
avocados, in Seven-Layer Dip, 47

B

Baby Shower menu, 182
bacon:
  Corn Chowder, 56
  and Garlic Green Beans, Cameron's, 112
  Macaroni and Cheese, 124
  Sheepherder's Skillet, 30, *31*
  Spinach-Artichoke Lasagne, 108
  Spinach Gouda Quiche, 32

Whiskey Brownies, Wayne's, 153
  -Wrapped Dates, 43
  -Wrapped Meatloaf, *90*, 91
  Zucchini with Onions, Jalapeño and, over Mashed Potatoes, Debbie's, 117
baking pans, greasing, 5
Balsamic Reduction, 65
banana(s):
  Bread Baked Oatmeal, 25
  Laurie's Cookie "Salad," 132
Bark, White Chocolate, *158*, 159
barley, in Taco Soup, 59
Bars, Lemon Shortbread, with Streusel Topping, 154, *155*
BBQ:
  Father's Day Barbecue menu, 182
  Pulled Pork Sandwiches, 95
  Southwest Chicken Salad, 78
bean(s):
  Black, and Chicken Enchiladas, Debbie's, 80–81
  Black, Soup, Spicy, 62
  refried, in Seven-Layer Dip, 47
  Taco Soup, 59
beef:
  Bacon-Wrapped Meatloaf, *90*, 91
  Borscht, Debbie's Mom's, 54
  Cheeseburger Soup, 57
  Guinness Pot Pie, 88–89, *89*

beef (*cont.*):
 Mozzarella-Stuffed
  Meatballs, 93
 Standing Rib Roast, 94
 Steak Sliders, Caramelized
  Onion, 85
beets, in Debbie's Mom's
 Borscht, 54
berry(ies):
 Triple, Crisp Baked
  Oatmeal, 25
 see also specific berries
beverages, *see* drinks
Biscotti, Almond, 145
Biscuits and Gravy, 26–27
black bean(s):
 and Chicken Enchiladas,
  Debbie's, 80–81
 Soup, Spicy, 62
 Taco Soup, 59
Blackberry-Lime Mojito, 167
black tea leaves:
 Christmas Spice Tea, 174, *175*
 Rosy Black Tea, 176
blueberry(ies):
 Crumb Cake, *12*, 13
 dried, in White Chocolate
  Bark, *158*, 159
Borscht, Debbie's Mom's, 54
Boston Cream Pie Poke Cake,
 138–39, *139*
breads:
 Chocolate Cherry Quick, 10
 Gratitude, *8*, 9
 No-Knead Dutch Oven, 126
breakfast, 7–33
 Apple Butter, Debbie's, 33
 Bacon Spinach Gouda
  Quiche, 32
 Baked Oatmeal, *24*, 25
 Biscuits and Gravy, 26–27
 Blueberry Crumb Cake, *12*, 13
 Chocolate Cherry Quick
  Bread, 10
 Chocolate Cranberry Croissant
  Pudding, 22
 Cinnamon Streusel Coffee
  Coffee Cake, 11
 Cream Cheese Danishes, 21
 Gratitude Bread, *8*, 9
 Lemon Ricotta Pancakes, 23
 Maple Pecan Scones with Bacon
  Maple Butter, 20

Muffin Tin Donut Holes,
 16, 17
 Overnight Caramel Pecan Rolls,
  14, *15*
 Pumpkin Apple Crunch
  Muffins, 18
 Sheepherder's Skillet, 30, *31*
 Strawberries and Cream Scones
  with Strawberry Butter, 19
 Tomato, Egg, and Prosciutto
  Tarts, *28*, 29
Breakfast for Dinner menu, 183
Broccoli Apple Cheddar Salad,
 66, 67
brownies:
 Chocolate Peppermint Trifle,
  134, 135
 Whiskey Bacon, Wayne's, 153
brunch:
 Mother's Day or Wedding
  Brunch menu, 182
 see also breakfast
buffets: All-Day Christmas Buffet,
 182
Business Meeting menu, 184
butter, 3
 Bacon Maple, 20
 greasing baking pans or muffin
  tins with, 5
 Sweet and Spicy, *114*, 115
buttercream frostings:
 Lemon Zest, *142*, 143–44
 Whiskey Bacon, 153
buttermilk biscuits, refrigerated,
 in Garlic Pizza Knots with
 Tomato Dipping Sauce,
 36, 37

C

cabbage:
 Borscht, Debbie's Mom's, 54
 Crunchy Ramen Salad
  with Honey-Ginger
  Vinaigrette, 68
Caesar Salad, Kale, 64
cakes:
 Blueberry Crumb, *12*, 13
 Boston Cream Pie Poke,
  138–39, *139*
 Cannoli Icebox, 133
 Caramel Apple Upside-Down,
  136, *137*

Cinnamon Streusel Coffee
 Coffee, 11
Lemon Cupcakes with Lemon
 Zest Frosting, *142*, 143–44
White Chocolate Cheesecake
 with Strawberries, 140–41,
 141
Cannoli Icebox Cake, 133
caramel:
 Apple Upside-Down Cake,
  136, *137*
 Pecan Rolls, Overnight, 14, *15*
 Salted, Dark Chocolate Tart,
  Decadent, 163
 Salted, –Drizzled Popcorn,
  40–41
 Salted, Filling, Chocolate
  Thumbprints with, 148–49
Caramelized Onion Steak
 Sliders, 85
Carrot Ginger Soup, 51
cashews:
 Skillet Cookie, *150*, 151
 White Chocolate Bark, *158*,
  159
Casserole, Layered Beef
 Enchilada, 92
champagne, 165
Cheddar cheese:
 Bacon Macaroni and Cheese,
  124
 Broccoli Apple Salad, *66*, 67
 Garlic Stuffed Potatoes, 118,
  119
 Seven-Layer Dip, 47
 Sheepherder's Skillet, 30, *31*
 Snow on the Mountain, 84
cheese, 3
 Bacon Macaroni and, 124
 Goat, and Roasted Cherry
  Tomato Dip, Warm, *44*, 45
 Gouda Bacon Spinach
  Quiche, 32
 mascarpone, in Cannoli Icebox
  Cake, 133
 see also feta cheese; Monterey
  Jack cheese; mozzarella
  (cheese); Parmesan cheese;
  Swiss cheese
Cheeseburger Soup, 57
Cheesecake, White Chocolate,
 with Strawberries, 140–41,
 141

cherry(ies):
    Chocolate Quick Bread, 10
    dried, in White Chocolate
        Bark, *158*, 159
chicken:
    and Black Bean Enchiladas,
        Debbie's, 80–81
    Pitas, Greek, with Tzatziki
        Sauce, *82*, 82–83
    Salad, Curried, 76, *77*
    Slow Cooker Honey Garlic, 75
    Snow on the Mountain, 84
    Southwest BBQ, Salad, 78
    Spinach-Artichoke Lasagne,
        108
chickpeas, in Hummus, 46
chiles:
    Layered Beef Enchilada
        Casserole, 92
    Tomatillo Salsa, 42
Chipotle-Honey Oven-Roasted
    Ribs, 99
chocolate:
    Cherry Quick Bread, 10
    chips, in Cannoli Icebox Cake,
        133
    chips, in Renelle's Christmas
        Toffee, 157
    chips, in Skillet Cookie, *150*,
        151
    Christmas Fudge, 156, *158*
    Cookies and Cream Frozen
        Dessert, *130*, 131
    Cranberry Croissant
        Pudding, 22
    Dark, Salted Caramel Tart,
        Decadent, 163
    Espresso Cookies, 146, *147*
    Glaze, 138–39, *139*
    Peppermint Trifle, *134*, 135
    Thumbprints with Salted
        Caramel Filling, 148–49
    Whiskey Bacon Brownies,
        Wayne's, 153
    White, Bark, *158*, 159
    White, Cheesecake with
        Strawberries, 140–41, *141*
    White and Dark, –Drizzled
        Popcorn, *40*, 40–41
    White Hot, *178*, 179
chowders:
    Bacon Corn, 56
    Clam, Debbie's Light, 55

chow mein noodles, in Snow on
    the Mountain, 84
Christmas menus:
    All-Day Christmas Buffet, 182
    Christmas Progressive Dinner,
        185
    Debbie's Christmas Tea for
        Friends, 184
Christmas treats:
    Fudge, 156, *158*
    Spice Tea, 174, *175*
    Toffee, Renelle's, 157
cilantro:
    Lime Sauce, *72*, 73
    Tomatillo Salsa, 42
cinnamon:
    Apple Baked Oatmeal, 25
    Christmas Spice Tea, 174, *175*
    Muffin Tin Donut Holes,
        16, 17
    Streusel Coffee Coffee Cake, 11
Clam Chowder, Debbie's
    Light, 55
coconut:
    Skillet Cookie, *150*, 151
    Snow on the Mountain, 84
coffee:
    Chocolate Espresso Cookies,
        146, *147*
    Coffee Cake, Cinnamon
        Streusel, 11
Committee Meeting menu, 184
condiments:
    Apple Butter, Debbie's, 33
    Bacon Maple Butter, 20
    Strawberry Butter, 19
    Sweet and Spicy Butter, *114*,
        115
    see also dressings; sauces
confections:
    Christmas Fudge, 156, *158*
    Christmas Toffee, Renelle's,
        157
    White Chocolate Bark, *158*,
        159
cookie(s):
    Almond Biscotti, 145
    Chocolate Espresso, 146, *147*
    Chocolate Thumbprints with
        Salted Caramel Filling,
        148–49
    and Cream Frozen Dessert,
        130, 131

Eggnog, 152
    "Salad," Laurie's, 132
    Skillet, *150*, 151
cooking spray, greasing baking
    pans or muffin tins with, 5
Cool Whip, in Laurie's Cookie
    "Salad," 132
corn:
    Bacon Chowder, 56
    Grilled, with Sweet and Spicy
        Butter, *114*, 115
    Layered Beef Enchilada
        Casserole, 92
    Southwest BBQ Chicken
        Salad, 78
cranberry(ies), dried:
    Chocolate Croissant
        Pudding, 22
    Skillet Cookie, *150*, 151
    White Chocolate Bark, *158*,
        159
cream, 3
    Cookies and, Frozen Dessert,
        130, 131
    Whipped, 131
Cream Cheese Danishes, 21
crescent roll dough, in Cream
    Cheese Danishes, 21
Croissant Pudding, Chocolate
    Cranberry, 22
Crumb Cake, Blueberry, *12*, 13
Crunchy Ramen Salad
    with Honey-Ginger
    Vinaigrette, 68
crusts:
    Graham Cracker, 140
    Oreo, 131
    Pie, 161
    Shortbread, 154
cucumber, in Tzatziki Sauce,
    82, 83
cupcake liners, filling, 144
Cupcakes, Lemon, with Lemon
    Zest Frosting, *142*, 143–44
Curried Chicken Salad, 76, *77*

D
Danishes, Cream Cheese, 21
Date Night menu, 184
Dates, Bacon-Wrapped, 43
Day Before Thanksgiving Feast
    menu, 94, 181

Decadent Dark Chocolate Salted
Caramel Tart, 163
Deep-Dish Pizza, 104–5
desserts, 129–63
    Almond Biscotti, 145
    Boston Cream Pie Poke Cake,
        138–39, *139*
    Cannoli Icebox Cake, 133
    Caramel Apple Upside-Down
        Cake, 136, *137*
    Chocolate Espresso Cookies,
        146, *147*
    Chocolate Peppermint Trifle,
        134, 135
    Chocolate Thumbprints with
        Salted Caramel Filling,
        148–49
    Christmas Fudge, 156, *158*
    Christmas Toffee, Renelle's, 157
    Cookie "Salad," Laurie's, 132
    Cookies and Cream Frozen
        Dessert, *130*, 131
    Decadent Dark Chocolate Salted
        Caramel Tart, 163
    Eggnog Cookies, 152
    Lemon Cupcakes with Lemon
        Zest Frosting, *142*, 143–44
    Lemon Shortbread Bars with
        Streusel Topping, 154, *155*
    Marionberry Pie, *160*, 161–62
    Skillet Cookie, *150*, 151
    Whiskey Bacon Brownies,
        Wayne's, 153
    White Chocolate Bark, *158*,
        159
    White Chocolate Cheesecake
        with Strawberries, 140–41,
        141
Dijon-Rosemary Sauce, *96*, 97
Dipping Sauce, Tomato, *36*, 37
dips:
    Goat Cheese and Roasted
        Cherry Tomato, Warm,
        44, 45
    Hummus, 46
    Seven-Layer, 47
    Tomatillo Salsa, 42
Donut Holes, Muffin Tin, *16*, 17
dressings:
    Balsamic Reduction, 65
    Caesar, 64
    Honey-Ginger Vinaigrette, 68
    Southwest, 78

dried soup mixes, 58, 58–62
    Rainbow Lentil, *58*, 60, *61*
    Spicy Black Bean, 62
    Taco, 59
drinks, 165–79
    Blackberry-Lime Mojito, 167
    Christmas Spice Tea, 174, *175*
    Grapefruit Frosé, 170, *171*
    homemade teas, 173–77
    Lavender Lemonade, 166
    Minty Lavender Herb Tea, 177
    Rosy Black Tea, 176
    Summer Fruit Sangria, *168*,
        169
    White Hot Chocolate, *178*,
        179
Dutch Oven No-Knead Bread,
    126

E

edamame, in Crunchy Ramen
    Salad with Honey-Ginger
    Vinaigrette, 68
egg(s), 3
    Asparagus Tomato Quiche, 101
    Bacon Spinach Gouda
        Quiche, 32
    Tomato, and Prosciutto Tarts,
        28, 29
Eggnog Cookies, 152
Elegant Dinner for Special Guests
    menu, 183
enchilada(s):
    Casserole, Layered Beef, 92
    Chicken and Black Bean,
        Debbie's, 80–81
Espresso Chocolate Cookies, 146,
    147

F

Father's Day Barbecue menu, 182
feta (cheese):
    Greek Chicken Pitas with
        Tzatziki Sauce, *82*, 82–83
    Watermelon Salad with
        Balsamic Reduction, 65
fish:
    Garlic Salmon Pasta in a Spicy
        Cream Sauce, 74
    Grilled, Tacos with Cilantro-
        Lime Sauce, *72*, 73

flour, 3
Fries, Baked Polenta, 122
frostings:
    Chocolate Glaze, 138–39,
        139
    Eggnog, 152
    Lemon Zest Buttercream, *142*,
        143–44
    Whiskey Bacon Buttercream,
        153
Frozen Dessert, Cookies and
    Cream, *130*, 131
fudge:
    Christmas, 156, *158*
    Cookies and Cream Frozen
        Dessert, *130*, 131

G

garlic:
    and Bacon Green Beans,
        Cameron's, 112
    Cheddar Stuffed Potatoes, 118,
        119
    Pizza Knots with Tomato
        Dipping Sauce, *36*, 37
    Roasted, Hummus, 46
    roasting, 5
    Salmon Pasta in a Spicy Cream
        Sauce, 74
gifts and party favors:
    Almond Biscotti, 145
    Apple Butter, Debbie's, 33
    Blueberry Crumb Cake, *12*, 13
    Chocolate Cherry Quick
        Bread, 10
    Chocolate Espresso Cookies,
        146, *147*
    Christmas Fudge, 156, *158*
    Christmas Toffee, Renelle's, 157
    dried soup mixes, 58, 58–62
    Gratitude Bread, *8*, 9
    homemade teas, 173–77
    Overnight Caramel Pecan Rolls,
        14, *15*
    Savory and Sweet Popcorn, *40*,
        40–41
    Sweet and Salty Nuts, 39
    White Chocolate Bark, *158*,
        159
ginger:
    Carrot Soup, 51
    Honey Vinaigrette, 68

glazes:
  Chocolate, 138–39, *139*
  Maple, 20
  Vanilla, 19
Goat Cheese and Roasted Cherry
  Tomato Dip, Warm,
  44, 45
Gouda Bacon Spinach Quiche, 32
Graduation Party menu, 183
graham cracker(s):
  Cannoli Icebox Cake, 133
  crust, 140
Granola Baked Oatmeal, 25
Grapefruit Frosé, 170, *171*
Gratitude Bread, *8, 9*
Gravy, 84
  Biscuits and, 26–27
greasing baking pans or muffin
  tins, 5
Greek Chicken Pitas with Tzatziki
  Sauce, *82,* 82–83
Green Beans, Garlic and Bacon,
  Cameron's, 112
green onions, 3
grilled:
  Corn with Sweet and Spicy
    Butter, *114,* 115
  Fish Tacos with Cilantro-Lime
    Sauce, *72, 73*
  Southwest BBQ Chicken
    Salad, 78
Gruyère cheese, in Caramelized
  Onion Steak Sliders, 85
Guinness Pot Pie, 88–89, *89*

H
hash browns, in Sheepherder's
  Skillet, 30, *31*
hazelnuts, in Skillet Cookie, *150,*
  151
herb(ed)(s):
  drying, 173
  Italian, Popcorn, 40–41
  Roasted Lamb Chops with
    Dijon-Rosemary Sauce,
    96, 97
  Rosy Black Tea, 176
  Tea, Minty Lavender, 177
  teas, making your own, 173
honey:
  Chipotle Oven-Roasted
    Ribs, 99

Garlic Slow Cooker Chicken, 75
Ginger Vinaigrette, 68
Hot Chocolate, White, *178,* 179
Hummus, 46

I
Icebox Cake, Cannoli, 133
ice cream, vanilla, in Cookies and
  Cream Frozen Dessert, *130,*
  131
ingredients, 3
Italian flavors:
  Almond Biscotti, 145
  Cannoli Icebox Cake, 133
  Deep-Dish Pizza, 104–5
  Garlic Pizza Knots with Tomato
    Dipping Sauce, *36, 37*
  Herbed Popcorn, 40–41
  Mozzarella-Stuffed Meatballs, 93
  Salami and Spinach Stromboli,
    102, *103*
  Spare Rib Spaghetti, Lacombe's,
    79
  Spinach-Artichoke Lasagne,
    108

J
Jalapeño, Zucchini with Bacon,
  Onions and, over Mashed
  Potatoes, Debbie's, 117

K
Kalamata Olive Hummus, 46
kale:
  Caesar Salad, 64
  Sausage, and Potato Soup,
    52, 53

L
Lacombe's Spare Rib Spaghetti, 79
Lamb Chops, Herb Roasted, with
  Dijon-Rosemary Sauce, *96,*
  97
Lasagne, Spinach-Artichoke, 108
Laurie's Cookie "Salad," 132
Laurie's Rice, 123
lavender:
  Herb Tea, Minty, 177
  Lemonade, 166

Layered Beef Enchilada
  Casserole, 92
lemon:
  Cupcakes with Lemon Zest
    Frosting, 142, 143–44
  Ricotta Pancakes, 23
  Shortbread Bars with Streusel
    Topping, 154, *155*
Lemonade, Lavender, 166
lemon balm, in Minty Lavender
  Herb Tea, 177
Lentil Soup, Rainbow, *58,* 60, *61*
Lettuce Wraps, Turkey, *86,* 87
lime:
  Blackberry Mojito, 167
  Cilantro Sauce, *72, 73*
Lunch for Friends menu, 184

M
macadamia nuts, in Skillet
  Cookie, *150,* 151
Macaroni and Cheese, Bacon, 124
mains, 71–108
  Asparagus Tomato Quiche, 101
  Bacon-Wrapped Meatloaf,
    90, 91
  Caramelized Onion Steak
    Sliders, 85
  Chicken and Black Bean
    Enchiladas, Debbie's, 80–81
  Curried Chicken Salad, 76, *77*
  Deep-Dish Pizza, 104–5
  Garlic Salmon Pasta in a Spicy
    Cream Sauce, 74
  Greek Chicken Pitas with
    Tzatziki Sauce, *82,* 82–83
  Grilled Fish Tacos with
    Cilantro-Lime Sauce, *72, 73*
  Guinness Pot Pie, 88–89, *89*
  Herb Roasted Lamb Chops
    with Dijon-Rosemary Sauce,
    96, 97
  Honey-Chipotle Oven-Roasted
    Ribs, 99
  Honey Garlic Chicken, Slow
    Cooker, 75
  Layered Beef Enchilada
    Casserole, 92
  Mozzarella-Stuffed Meatballs, 93
  Peanut Butter Noodles with
    Thai Flavors and Crispy Tofu,
    106, 107

mains (*cont.*):
    Pulled Pork, Easy Slow
      Cooker, 95
    Salami and Spinach Stromboli,
      102, *103*
    Snow on the Mountain, 84
    Southwest BBQ Chicken
      Salad, 78
    Spare Rib Spaghetti,
      Lacombe's, 79
    Spicy Pork Chops, 98
    Spinach-Artichoke Lasagne,
      108
    Standing Rib Roast, 94
    Turkey Lettuce Wraps, *86*, 87
mandarin oranges, in Crunchy
    Ramen Salad with Honey-
    Ginger Vinaigrette, 68
M&Ms, in White Chocolate
    Bark, *158*, 159
Maple Pecan Scones with Bacon
    Maple Butter, 20
Marionberry Pie, *160*, 161–62
marshmallows, in Christmas
    Fudge, 156, *158*
mascarpone cheese, in Cannoli
    Icebox Cake, 133
measurements, 5
Meatballs, Mozzarella-Stuffed, 93
Meatloaf, Bacon-Wrapped, *90*, 91
menus:
    All-Day Christmas Buffet, 182
    Baby Shower, 182
    Breakfast for Dinner, 183
    Date Night, 184
    Day Before Thanksgiving Feast,
      94, 181
    Debbie's Christmas Tea for
      Friends, 184
    Elegant Dinner for Special
      Guests, 183
    Father's Day Barbecue, 182
    Lunch for Friends/Committee/
      Business Meeting, 184
    Mother's Day or Wedding
      Brunch, 182
    Perfect Potluck Dinner, 183
    Summer Picnic, 184
    Sweet Sixteen/Graduation
      Party, 183
Mexican and Tex-Mex flavors:
    Chicken and Black Bean
      Enchiladas, Debbie's, 80–81

Grilled Fish Tacos with
    Cilantro-Lime Sauce, *72*, 73
Layered Beef Enchilada
    Casserole, 92
Seven-Layer Dip, 47
Spicy Black Bean Soup, 62
Taco Soup, 59
Tomatillo Salsa, 42
milk, 3
mint(y):
    Blackberry-Lime Mojito, 167
    Lavender Herb Tea, 177
Mojito, Blackberry-Lime, 167
Monterey Jack cheese:
    Bacon Macaroni and Cheese,
      124
    Seven-Layer Dip, 47
    Spinach-Artichoke Lasagne,
      108
Mother's Day Brunch menu, 182
mozzarella (cheese):
    Deep-Dish Pizza, 104–5
    Salami and Spinach Stromboli,
      102, *103*
    -Stuffed Meatballs, 93
Muffins, Pumpkin Apple
    Crunch, 18
Muffin Tin Donut Holes, *16*, 17
muffin tins, greasing, 5
mushroom(s):
    and Caramelized Onion
      Bites, 38
    Guinness Pot Pie, 88–89, *89*
    Turkey Lettuce Wraps, *86*, 87

N

Nachos, Pulled Pork, 95
nectarines, in Summer
    Fruit Sangria, *168*,
    169
No-Knead Dutch Oven Bread,
    126
noodle(s):
    chow mein, in Snow on the
      Mountain, 84
    Crunchy Ramen Salad
      with Honey-Ginger
      Vinaigrette, 68
    Peanut Butter, with Thai
      Flavors and Crispy Tofu,
      106, 107
    see also pasta

nuts:
    Sweet and Salty, 39
    toasting, 5
    see also specific nuts

O

Oatmeal, Baked, *24*, 25
olive(s), black:
    Kalamata, Hummus, 46
    kalamata, in Southwest BBQ
      Chicken Salad, 78
    Layered Beef Enchilada
      Casserole, 92
    Seven-Layer Dip, 47
    Snow on the Mountain, 84
onion(s):
    Caramelized, and Mushroom
      Bites, 38
    Caramelized, Steak Sliders, 85
    volume measurements for, 5
orange(s):
    mandarin, in Crunchy Ramen
      Salad with Honey-Ginger
      Vinaigrette, 68
    peel, drying, 174
Oreo Crust, 131
Overnight Caramel Pecan Rolls,
    14, *15*

P

Pancakes, Lemon Ricotta, 23
Parmesan cheese:
    Garlic Salmon Pasta in a Spicy
      Cream Sauce, 74
    Mushroom and Caramelized
      Onion Bites, 38
    Popcorn, *40*, 40–41
    Rolls, Debbie's Grandkids', 125
    Spinach-Artichoke Lasagne,
      108
party favors, *see* gifts and party
    favors
pasta:
    Bacon Macaroni and Cheese,
      124
    Garlic Salmon, in a Spicy
      Cream Sauce, 74
    Spare Rib Spaghetti,
      Lacombe's, 79
    Spinach-Artichoke Lasagne,
      108

peaches, in Summer Fruit Sangria, *168*, 169
Peanut Butter Noodles with Thai Flavors and Crispy Tofu, *106*, 107
pecan:
　Caramel, Rolls, Overnight, 14, *15*
　Maple Scones with Bacon Maple Butter, 20
pepper, 3
pepper(s), red:
　Roasted, Hummus, 46
　Southwest BBQ Chicken Salad, 78
Peppermint Chocolate Trifle, *134*, 135
pepperoni:
　Deep-Dish Pizza, 104–5
　Garlic Pizza Knots with Tomato Dipping Sauce, *36*, 37
Perfect Potluck Dinner menu, 183
picnics: Summer Picnic menu, 184
pies:
　Guinness Pot, 88–89, *89*
　Marionberry, *160*, 161–62
pineapple:
　Laurie's Cookie "Salad," 132
　Snow on the Mountain, 84
pistachios, in White Chocolate Bark, *158*, 159
Pitas, Greek Chicken, with Tzatziki Sauce, *82*, 82–83
pizza (dough):
　Knots, Garlic, with Tomato Dipping Sauce, *36*, 37
　making, 104
　Salami and Spinach Stromboli, 102, *103*
Pizza, Deep-Dish, 104–5
plums, in Summer Fruit Sangria, *168*, 169
Poke Cake, Boston Cream Pie, 138–39, *139*
Polenta Fries, Baked, 122
Popcorn, Savory and Sweet, *40*, 40–41
pork:
　Chops, Spicy, 98
　ground beef and, in Bacon-Wrapped Meatleaf, *90*, 91
　Pulled, Easy Slow Cooker, 95

Ribs, Honey-Chipotle Oven-Roasted, 99
Spare Rib Spaghetti, Lacombe's, 79
see also bacon; sausage
potato(es):
　Borscht, Debbie's Mom's, 54
　Cheddar Garlic Stuffed, 118, *119*
　Cheeseburger Soup, 57
　Guinness Pot Pie, 88–89, *89*
　hash browns, in Sheepherder's Skillet, 30, *31*
　Mashed, Debbie's Zucchini with Bacon, Onions, and Jalapeño over, 117
　Salad, Adler, *120*, 121
　Sausage, and Kale Soup, *52*, 53
Potluck Dinner menu, 183
Pot Pie, Guinness, 88–89, *89*
Prosciutto, Tomato, and Egg Tarts, *28*, 29
Pudding, Chocolate Cranberry Croissant, 22
pudding mix, vanilla:
　Boston Cream Pie Poke Cake, 138–39, *139*
　Chocolate Peppermint Trifle, *134*, 135
　Laurie's Cookie "Salad," 132
puff pastry:
　Guinness Pot Pie, 88–89, *89*
　Mushroom and Caramelized Onion Bites, 38
　Tomato, Egg, and Prosciutto Tarts, *28*, 29
Pulled Pork, Easy Slow Cooker, 95
Pumpkin Apple Crunch Muffins, 18

Q
quiches:
　Asparagus Tomato, 101
　Bacon Spinach Gouda, 32

R
Rainbow Lentil Soup, *58*, 60, *61*
Ramen, Crunchy, Salad with Honey-Ginger Vinaigrette, 68

refried beans, in Seven-Layer Dip, 47
refrigerator doughs:
　buttermilk biscuit, in Garlic Pizza Knots with Tomato Dipping Sauce, *36*, 37
　crescent roll, in Cream Cheese Danishes, 21
Renelle's Christmas Toffee, 157
Ribs, Honey-Chipotle Oven-Roasted, 99
rice:
　Laurie's, 123
　Snow on the Mountain, 84
Ricotta Lemon Pancakes, 23
rolls:
　Debbie's Grandkids', 125
　Overnight Caramel Pecan, 14, *15*
rosé, in Grapefruit Frosé, 170, *171*
Rosemary-Dijon Sauce, *96*, 97
Rosy Black Tea, 176
rum, in Blackberry-Lime Mojito, 167

S
salads, 63–68
　Broccoli Apple Cheddar, *66*, 67
　Crunchy Ramen, with Honey-Ginger Vinaigrette, 68
　Curried Chicken, 76, *77*
　Kale Caesar, 64
　Potato, Adler, *120*, 121
　Southwest BBQ Chicken, 78
　Watermelon Feta, with Balsamic Reduction, 65
Salami and Spinach Stromboli, 102, *103*
Salmon Garlic Pasta in a Spicy Cream Sauce, 74
Salsa, Tomatillo, 42
salt, 3
salted caramel:
　Dark Chocolate Tart, Decadent, 163
　–Drizzled Popcorn, 40–41
　Filling, Chocolate Thumbprints with, 148–49
Sandwiches, BBQ Pulled Pork, 95
Sangria, Summer Fruit, *168*, 169

sauces:
Cilantro-Lime, *72*, 73
Dijon-Rosemary, 96, 97
Tomato Dipping Sauce, *36*, 37
Tzatziki, *82*, 83
sausage:
Kale, and Potato Soup, *52*, 53
Mozzarella-Stuffed
Meatballs, 93
pork, in Biscuits and Gravy,
26–27
Savory and Sweet Popcorn, *40*,
40–41
scallions, 3
scones:
Maple Pecan, with Bacon
Maple Butter, 20
Strawberries and Cream, with
Strawberry Butter, 19
Seven-Layer Dip, 47
Sheepherder's Skillet, 30, *31*
Shortbread Bars, Lemon, with
Streusel Topping, 154, *155*
sides, 111–26
Bacon Macaroni and Cheese,
124
Baked Polenta Fries, 122
Cheddar Garlic Stuffed
Potatoes, 118, *119*
Garlic and Bacon Green Beans,
Cameron's, 112
Grilled Corn with Sweet and
Spicy Butter, *114*, 115
No-Knead Dutch Oven Bread,
126
Potato Salad, Adler, *120*, 121
Rice, Laurie's, 123
Roasted Sesame Asparagus, 116
Rolls, Debbie's Grandkids', 125
Zucchini with Bacon, Onions,
and Jalapeño over Mashed
Potatoes, Debbie's, 117
skillet:
Cookie, *150*, 151
Sheepherder's, 30, *31*
Sliders, Caramelized Onion
Steak, 85
slow cooker:
Honey Garlic Chicken, 75
Pulled Pork, Easy, 95
Spare Rib Spaghetti,
Lacombe's, 79

snacks, *see* appetizers and snacks
Snow on the Mountain, 84
soups, 49–62
Bacon Corn Chowder, 56
Borscht, Debbie's Mom's, 54
Carrot Ginger, 51
Cheeseburger, 57
Clam Chowder, Debbie's
Light, 55
dried soup mixes, *58*, 58–62
Rainbow Lentil, *58*, 60, *61*
Sausage, Kale, and Potato,
52, 53
Spicy Black Bean, 62
Taco, 59
Southwest BBQ Chicken
Salad, 78
Spaghetti, Spare Rib,
Lacombe's, 79
spare rib(s):
Honey-Chipotle Oven-
Roasted, 99
Spaghetti, Lacombe's, 79
Spice Tea, Christmas, 174, *175*
Spicy, Sweet, and Salty Nuts, 39
Spicy Black Bean Soup, 62
Spicy Pork Chops, 98
spinach:
Artichoke Lasagne, 108
Bacon Gouda Quiche, 32
and Salami Stromboli, 102, *103*
Standing Rib Roast, 94
Steak Sliders, Caramelized
Onion, 85
strawberries:
and Cream Scones with
Strawberry Butter, 19
White Chocolate Cheesecake
with, 140–41, *141*
Streusel Topping, 11, 154
Stromboli, Salami and Spinach,
102, *103*
sugar, 3
Summer Fruit Sangria, *168*,
169
Sweet and Salty Nuts, 39
Sweet and Spicy Butter, *114*, 115
Sweet Sixteen Party menu, 183
Swiss cheese:
Asparagus Tomato Quiche, 101
Caramelized Onion Steak
Sliders, 85

T
taco(s):
Grilled Fish, with Cilantro-
Lime Sauce, *72*, 73
Pulled Pork, 95
Soup, 59
tarts:
Asparagus Tomato Quiche, 101
Bacon Spinach Gouda
Quiche, 32
Decadent Dark Chocolate
Salted Caramel, 163
Tomato, Egg, and Prosciutto,
28, 29
teas, homemade, 173–77
best herbs for, 173
Christmas Spice, 174, *175*
drying herbs for, 173
Minty Lavender Herb, 177
Rosy Black, 176
Tex-Mex flavors, *see* Mexican and
Tex-Mex flavors
Thanksgiving:
Day Before Thanksgiving Feast
menu, 94, 181
serving appetizers on, 35
Thumbprints, Chocolate, with
Salted Caramel Filling,
148–49
toffee:
bits, in Skillet Cookie, *150*, 151
Christmas, Renelle's, 157
Tofu, Crispy, Peanut Butter
Noodles with Thai Flavors
and, *106*, 107
Tomatillo Salsa, 42
tomato(es):
Asparagus Quiche, 101
Dipping Sauce, *36*, 37
Egg, and Prosciutto Tarts,
28, 29
Roasted Cherry, and Goat
Cheese Dip, Warm, *44*, 45
Seven-Layer Dip, 47
Tomatillo Salsa, 42
tortilla(s):
Chicken and Black Bean
Enchiladas, Debbie's, 80–81
chips, in Pulled Pork Tacos, 95
Grilled Fish Tacos with
Cilantro-Lime Sauce,
72, 73

Layered Beef Enchilada
    Casserole, 92
Pulled Pork Tacos, 95
strips or chips, in Southwest
    BBQ Chicken Salad, 78
Trifle, Chocolate Peppermint,
    134, 135
Triple Berry Crisp Baked
    Oatmeal, 25
Turkey Lettuce Wraps, *86*, 87
Tzatziki Sauce, *82*, 83

U

Upside-Down Cake, Caramel
    Apple, 136, *137*

V

vanilla ice cream, in Cookies and
    Cream Frozen Dessert, *130*,
    131
vanilla pudding mix:
    Boston Cream Pie Poke Cake,
        138–39, *139*

Chocolate Peppermint Trifle,
    134, 135
Laurie's Cookie "Salad," 132
vegetable oil, 3
Velveeta, in Cheeseburger Soup, 57
Vinaigrette, Honey-Ginger, 68

W

walnuts, in Skillet Cookie, *150*,
    151
water chestnuts, in Turkey
    Lettuce Wraps, *86*, 87
Watermelon Feta Salad with
    Balsamic Reduction, 65
Wayne's Whiskey Bacon Brownies,
    153
Wedding Brunch menu, 182
Whipped Cream, 131
Whiskey Bacon Brownies,
    Wayne's, 153
white chocolate:
    Bark, *158*, 159
    Cheesecake with Strawberries,
        140–41, *141*

chips, in Chocolate Peppermint
    Trifle, *134*, 135
chips, in Skillet Cookie, *150*,
    151
and Dark Chocolate–Drizzled
    Popcorn, *40*, 40–41
Hot Chocolate, *178*, 179
wine:
    collecting, 165
    red, in Summer Fruit Sangria,
        168, 169
    rosé, in Grapefruit Frosé, 170,
        171
Wraps, Turkey Lettuce, *86*, 87

Y

yogurt, in Tzatziki Sauce,
    82, 83

Z

Zucchini with Bacon, Onions,
    and Jalapeño over Mashed
    Potatoes, Debbie's, 117

ABOUT THE AUTHOR

DEBBIE MACOMBER, the author of *Any Dream Will Do, If Not for You, Sweet Tomorrows, A Girl's Guide to Moving On, Last One Home, Silver Linings, Love Letters, Mr. Miracle, Blossom Street Brides,* and *Rose Harbor in Bloom,* is a leading voice in women's fiction. Thirteen of her novels have reached #1 on the *New York Times* bestseller lists, and five of her beloved Christmas novels have been hit movies on the Hallmark Channel, including *Mrs. Miracle* and *Mr. Miracle.* Hallmark Channel also produced the original series *Debbie Macomber's Cedar Cove,* based on Macomber's Cedar Cove books. She has more than 200 million copies of her books in print worldwide.

debbiemacomber.com

Facebook.com/debbiemacomberworld

Twitter: @debbiemacomber

Instagram: @debbiemacomber

Pinterest.com/macomberbooks

ABOUT THE TYPE

This book was set in Garamond, a typeface originally designed by the Parisian type cutter Claude Garamond (c. 1500–61). This version of Garamond was modeled on a 1592 specimen sheet from the Egenolff-Berner foundry, which was produced from types assumed to have been brought to Frankfurt by the punch cutter Jacques Sabon (c. 1520–80).

Claude Garamond's distinguished romans and italics first appeared in *Opera Ciceronis* in 1543–44. The Garamond types are clear, open, and elegant.